AIA New Jersey
Guidebook

AIA New Jersey Guidebook

150 Best Buildings and Places

Philip S. Kennedy-Grant, FAIA
Author, Editor

Mark Alan Hewitt, FAIA
Author

Michael J. Mills, FAIA
Author

Alexander M. Noble
Photographer

**Foreword by Michael Graves, FAIA,
with Karen Nichols, FAIA**

Rivergate Books
an imprint of
Rutgers University Press
New Brunswick, New Jersey, and London

Library of Congress Cataloging-in-Publication Data

AIA New Jersey guidebook : 150 best buildings and places / Philip S. Kennedy-
Grant, author, editor . . . [et al.].
     p.   cm.
    Includes bibliographical references and index.
    ISBN 978-0-8135-5126-5 (pbk. : alk. paper)
    1. Architecture—New Jersey—Guidebooks. I. Kennedy-Grant, Philip S.
  II. American Institute of Architects. III. Title : American Institute of
Architects New Jersey guidebook.
    NA730.N36A39 2011
    720.9749—dc22
                                 2010048425

A British Cataloging-in-Publication record for this book is available from the
British Library.

Visit our Web site: http://rutgerspress.rutgers.edu

Manufactured in Singapore

Contents

Foreword: Telling Stories in New Jersey
by Michael Graves with Karen Nichols   vii

Acknowledgments   ix

Introduction   1

1   The Gateway Region   7

2   The Shore Region   75

3   The Greater Atlantic City Region
      and Southern Shore Region   107

4   The Delaware River Region   134

5   The Skylands Region   163

      Closing Thoughts   179

About the Authors   183
AIA New Jersey Contributors   185
Index   187

Foreword: Telling Stories in New Jersey

As this fascinating book reveals, the architecture of New Jersey contains a great diversity of contexts and intentions, and also a remarkable richness and high quality of design. The architecture of any place embodies not only its history but also its social and cultural values. New Jerseyans have commissioned and created buildings and places of character for centuries and have striven to preserve the architectural heritage and important landscapes within this small but dense state. Architects today certainly appreciate this, and I am sure that anyone interested in architecture, places, and history will be as taken with the photographs and descriptions in this book as my colleagues and I are.

When I moved to New Jersey in 1962 to teach architecture at Princeton University, and eventually established my architecture and design practices in Princeton, I became intrigued by the many stories and layers of history that this town—and all of New Jersey—reveal. New Jersey is a distinctly American place, certainly because of its role in the American Revolution, and also because it encompasses a wide and diverse spectrum of people and places. The state's varied physical environment—from the Sourland Mountains to the Jersey Shore, from the Palisades to the Meadowlands—contributes to a localized sense of place, and much of the architecture follows suit. The organization of this book into geographical regions thus focuses attention on the relationship between buildings and the natural or urban landscapes that form their contexts.

Like the variations in the land, the range of buildings represented here is simply amazing: the hoopla of the Jersey Shore, classically inspired libraries, museums, courthouses, and monuments of civic importance, former industrial sites rendered picturesque as ruins, and highly personalized and sometimes quirky private residences, to name just a few types. Although only 150 examples were selected—in honor of the 150th anniversary of the American Institute of Architects—Philip Kennedy-Grant rightly points out that historians and the architectural community could easily identify many more, revealing an even greater breadth of New Jersey's built and natural environment.

What I find most compelling about this book, in addition to Sandy Noble's stunning photographs, are the descriptions of the buildings and places written by Kennedy-Grant, Mark Hewitt, and Michael Mills. Not merely captions with historical facts, these texts contain intriguing, insightful, and informative stories. Some are stories about architects' intentions and inventiveness, their response to the context, and the influence of their designs on future generations. Some capture the aspirations of the clients and how their particular visions became reflected in the buildings and places they commissioned. Other stories address the social milieu, the building of communities, the commemoration of events, and our seasonal rituals. And still others celebrate the landscape, the natural and built places of the Garden State, paying tribute to our native geography and our citizens' love of the outdoors. This multifaceted approach captures the spirit of the diverse experiences that characterize New Jersey.

Finally, I congratulate AIA New Jersey and all of the contributors for conceiving of this book and producing it with such thoughtfulness, scholarship, and beauty. Through its stories and photographs, it fulfills its mission to increase the understanding of New Jersey architecture and places, and piques our curiosity to know more about the rich history of our surroundings.

Michael Graves, FAIA
with Karen Nichols, FAIA

Acknowledgments

Pretty much the best of everything happens in collaboration. Even the solitary poet requires a reader. A production such as this occurs due to the talents of dozens of people. The instigator for the book was Martin Santini, FAIA—it was a brilliant idea. The man whose cause and responsibility it became is Edward N. Rothe, FAIA. He has been a wise and encouraging shepherd. The AIA New Jersey committee members and individual contributors are listed at the end of the book. Their thoughtful recommendations produced the list of 150 places this book documents. The AIA New Jersey officers have been uniformly supportive and patient. I am delighted and lucky to work with Marlie Wasserman and her staff at Rutgers University Press. Their enthusiasm for the book and their ever-present knowledge and optimism provided emotional, technical, and practical support when it was most needed. I could not have better co-writers and collaborators than Mark A. Hewitt, FAIA, Michael J. Mills, FAIA, and Sandy Noble. Mark and Michael know virtually everything there is to know about the architectural history of New Jersey, and their ability to condense the breadth of their knowledge into brief descriptions is laudable. Sandy took every photograph you see and hundreds more besides. He visited sites multiple times, cheerfully, to capture the images the editor imagined could be. Scores of other individuals have been keen supporters, particularly those whose buildings we have visited. They invited us into homes, allowed their workplaces to be interrupted, helped direct traffic, removed storm windows, and otherwise selflessly expressed support that, at every turn, made our work easier and more enjoyable. Finally, great credit is due Elizabeth Faulkner, whose tireless dedication to this effort has ensured its success. Her critical eye is accompanied by a thoughtfulness and generosity of spirit that is incalculable as well as unmatched. This is a pretty darn good little book. My heartfelt thanks to all of you who have helped make it so.

Philip S. Kennedy-Grant, FAIA

AIA New Jersey
Guidebook

Introduction

This book grew out of the idea to celebrate 150 years of the American Institute of Architects in New Jersey. In 2007 the New Jersey chapter asked its members to make suggestions of the best buildings and places in New Jersey. Not surprisingly, recommendations came from architects all across the state. A committee was formed to catalogue these recommendations and compile a list of the top 150. The fruits of that effort are contained in these pages.

The American Institute of Architects is the country's preeminent professional organization of architects. Founded in 1857 in New York City, spearheaded by Richard Upjohn and including Richard Morris Hunt, the first American graduate of France's École des Beaux Arts, the group gathered to address concerns over their nascent profession. Of particular interest, they wanted to "elevate the standing of the profession as well as promote the scientific and practical perfection of its members." Their numbers grew quickly, with chapters established across the country by 1887. Since that initial meeting of thirteen individuals, the society has grown to 86,000 members. At first glance, that may seem to be a large number, but it represents less than one-half of one percent of the country's population. The New Jersey chapter today numbers only 2,066 members.

New Jersey is an architecturally rich state, but very little information exists to document that richness. This volume represents the first conscientious, statewide, pictorial treatment of New Jersey architecture in many years. And although it is not purely historical in scope, it does begin to shed light on the breadth, diversity, and excellence of our state's architecture. We hope that when the casual reader visits a particular site he/she will be moved enough to pursue further investigation and research.

As in many collective endeavors, the definition of standards can be elusive, particularly when trying to describe the "best." In attempting to categorize buildings and places, what parts age, idiosyncrasy, occupants, and ownership play in the definition will vary, as will more subjective categories such as style, intention, and significance. Gatherings of confident, independent professionals rarely issue uncontested opinions. That is the case here.

There are clearly monumental and architecturally unassailable buildings included in this volume, doubtlessly considered among the best in the state. Just as clearly, the selection of others may raise an eyebrow. This is to be expected. What it illustrates is the variety of strong, and strongly argued, opinions present within our borders. Democracy is messy. And getting anything constructed worthy of being known as architecture is hard work, in which compromise is a constant. It may be that the arguments generated by that which has been included, and that which has been left out, will foster further discussion about the "best" buildings and places, and lead to revisions and future editions of this exercise.

It is essential to look at buildings in order to learn how others have achieved, or failed to achieve, architectural success. How one looks at buildings is critical. It is easy to photograph them, and it has become very easy to take a lot of photographs. But photography is often a disconnected way of seeing. The focus can become too centered on the image created and lose sight of what makes the building worth considering. The photographs contained herein were all commissioned for this book. And although we show only one image for each project, in every instance multiple images were taken in an effort to capture, if not the essence, at least a suggestion of the character of the building or place. In several instances, multiple trips were taken to the sites in order to present a more compelling or revealing image.

This book is intended as a guide, an introduction to the wonderful breadth of New Jersey's architecture. It is laid out in chapters according to the broad geographic regions established by the New Jersey Department of

Skylands

Gateway

Shore

Delaware River

Greater Atlantic
City and Southern
Shore

Tourism (shown on the accompanying map). A summary of each region precedes its chapter entries. The regions are presented in a clockwise geographical pattern, beginning to the northeast, around the east to the south, and finally to the northwest. Within each region, the buildings follow the same approximate arrangement. The entries for the Gateway Region far exceed the number of examples from the other regions, principally as a result of its greater population density. The concentration of industry, commerce, and associated personal wealth spurred the construction of significant works of architecture.

When you visit a site with this book in hand, take a moment to consider the building in its setting, how it relates to its neighboring buildings, how it addresses the street. You might also pause to consider why a particular image was used. Do you see a better angle? Is there a more interesting detail? Is the image characteristic of the whole or is it only the best part? By considering these questions, you can begin to grasp how architecture acts upon us and start to develop an appreciation for good work. It is worth remembering, too, that this list was compiled by architects. Do architects see things in ways that others do not? Perhaps you perceive a pattern. We recognize that this is a first pass at the effort, but it may be of interest to discern tendencies illustrated by this list that do not align precisely with your own point of view.

This is not a history of New Jersey architecture, but an introduction to the history of the state's wonderful built environment. It is intended not only to celebrate good work, but also to pique interest in architecture and in how architecture is differentiated from mere buildings. Top to bottom, side to side, New Jersey has countless, marvelous examples of outstanding architecture.

We in the AIA are proud to have been part of the creation of that excellence over the past 150 years. It is an important and worthy exercise to assemble this list, and it is a cause for celebration that we have been able to have the choices photographed so marvelously for this publication.

The book illustrates quite clearly the diversity of our state's architecture. Both massive buildings and diminutive structures are included. Each has been selected because it exemplifies a segment of our culture and the care and thoughtfulness brought to bear by its architect to solve a specific spatial problem.

Many of the buildings are individual landmarks, but all are influenced by their surroundings. It is important to understand the impact that a building's immediate environment has on its creation and on how it is perceived. The grandeur of a civic structure in a large city is starkly contrasted with the intimacy and warmth of a private home in the country. And the enthusiasm and whimsy of our shoreline architecture, exemplified by Wildwood's Doo Wop buildings, is unmatched elsewhere.

You will note the inclusion of places as well as individual structures. Often the public spaces defined by urban blocks or the openness of parks provide opportunities for release and repose in our fast-paced culture. The inclusion of parks seems obvious, but communities with strong identities and active populations have no less strong a hold on our consciousness.

Finally, the excellence of New Jersey architecture can easily be imagined simply by listing architects who have completed work in the state: Ralph Adams Cram, McKim Mead and White, Carrère and Hastings, Frank Lloyd Wright, Eero Saarinen, Louis Kahn, Robert Venturi, Michael Graves, Richard Rogers. These are stars in the architectural firmament, but they are not alone. Work by lesser-known but no less accomplished architects, such as Marion Sims Wyeth and Guilbert and Betelle, is prevalent. And the efforts of countless unknown craftsmen/architects from New Jersey's earliest settlements are responsible for the beautiful and timeless design of houses, barns, meetinghouses, and churches that we admire and strive to protect today.

We are blessed to have an active and effective architectural conservation community in New Jersey, composed of architects, preservationists, historians, teachers, government employees, elected officials, and dedicated citizens, for whom the education of the public and the conservation of our architectural heritage are important social goals.

We are delighted to be able to present these buildings and places together in one volume, as a celebration of New Jersey's architectural excellence from its earliest days to the present. We hope you enjoy visiting them.

Ellis Island
PSK-G

1
The Gateway Region

The northeastern part of the state is its most densely populated area and operates in tension within the megalopolis that is New York City. Although there is clearly a tendency to think this region has simply been absorbed into New York's aura, the fact is that the Gateway Region very much has its own identity. The area was settled and became a success because of its excellent waterways. New York Harbor and the Hudson, Passaic, and Hackensack Rivers were all essential to the economic life of the region. Paterson's Great Falls was the founding site of America's industrial revolution, and the factories that bloomed throughout the region fed much of the nation's thirst for growth.

Chief among the area's historic assets are Ellis Island and Liberty State Park. It was through Ellis Island that millions of immigrants passed on their way toward becoming American citizens and enriching a culture already pulsing with diversity. The importance of this entrance to the immediate region cannot be overstated. The impact of such a diverse immigrant population on the character of the society, touching as it does our food, our speech, our music, our art, and our religions, is incalculable.

Though now crisscrossed by multilane highways, with their overpasses, bridges, and rampways, the region is still rife with handsome neighborhoods and vibrant towns. Newark is the center of this region, and though it continues to struggle to regain its former glory, architectural and cultural jewels like the New Jersey Performing Arts Center suggest that optimism for its future is well founded. Newark's Ironbound, the neighborhood defined by the railroad that transports thousands daily, is a polyglot community of Spanish, Portuguese, and Brazilian people, resoundingly celebrated for their regional cuisine. The Newark Museum is highly regarded across the country for its stellar collections, and the Montclair Art Museum is well known for its Hudson River School collection. Towns throughout the region expanded in the late nineteenth century with the proliferation of railroad lines and still contain many and varied examples of fine residential architecture in multiple styles.

Palisades Interstate Park

The Palisades run along the west bank of the Hudson River from the Rahway River across from Staten Island, north toward the Hudson Highlands of New York. The stretch in New Jersey from the George Washington Bridge to the New York border is impressive for its sheer cliffs rising as much as five hundred feet from the water's edge. Palisades Interstate Park contains 53,320 acres in eleven parcels across New Jersey and New York, and stretches along twenty-four miles of the Hudson's bank. The park was established in 1899, the result of concern for the devastation caused by quarries blasting for trap rock. As the demand for concrete for ever taller and more abundant skyscrapers in Manhattan increased, the public's concern became significant enough to thwart the quarrying activity. Following initial set-asides, additional lands have been donated to the park, which now stretches as far north as Haverstraw Bay and as far west as the Catskill Forest Preserve. Hiking trails have been established along the shoreline and atop the ridge, allowing visitors to enjoy the natural beauty of this stunning geologic feature.

Horizon House is a cluster of residential buildings, constructed from 1961 through 1968, situated on thirty-two acres in Fort Lee. The development includes four fourteen-story structures, designed by the firm of Kelly and Gruzen, and two twenty-eight story towers, designed by Bruce Graham and Natalie de Blois of Skidmore, Owings and Merrill. Graham later designed the John Hancock Center and Sears Tower (now Willis Tower) in Chicago, while de Blois was one of the most prominent female architects involved in commercial practice in mid-twentieth-century America. This project is significant because it concentrated mid-rise and tall structures, more typically associated with dense urban sites, in a parklike setting, with views overlooking the Hudson River. It is an early example of attempts to maximize a property's density while making efforts to incorporate qualities of community. In this respect, it adapts aspects of Le Corbusier's ideas about city planning, most notably illustrated in his design for Ville Radieuse. Unusual for their time, the four lower, mid-rise buildings by Kelly and Gruzen are designed with duplex and through-floor apartments. The elevators stop at every other floor. The atypical interior permitted the façades to be designed in a more interesting and varied way.

No less a luminary than Le Corbusier called the George Washington Bridge the most beautiful in the world, and many agree with him. If it suffers somewhat by comparison with its neighbors in Brooklyn and Staten Island, the "GW" is still a superstar in the world of bridge design. It was the first independent work of Othmar H. Ammann (1879–1965), one of the greatest of all bridge designers, who had a long engineering career in and around New York City. While working as an assistant to Gustav Lindenthal, the renowned designer of the Hell Gate arch bridge for the Pennsylvania Railroad, Ammann first became intrigued with the idea of a span over the Hudson River to link Manhattan Island with New Jersey. In the early 1920s, his mentor unsuccessfully promoted a bridge that would cross the river at Fifty-seventh Street. Sensing that this scheme was flawed, Ammann left Lindenthal to form his own engineering firm. He promptly designed a suspension bridge that would span a shorter distance, using elevated anchorages on the Palisades at Fort Lee and bluffs above 179th Street. In 1927 the Port of New York Authority (later the Port Authority of New York and New Jersey) hired him to design the bridge he had already envisioned. Finished in 1931, the graceful steel structure measured 4,760 feet between anchorages and featured two 635-foot towers with distinctive cross braces. The consulting architect, Cass Gilbert, is never mentioned in descriptions of the GWB, for here the engineer's aesthetic prevailed. Ammann went on to design numerous bridges in and around New York, including the Bronx-Whitestone Bridge and the Verrazano-Narrows Bridge.

Erected in 1927, the Ridgefield Park railroad station once accommodated 25,000 passengers a day on the line from West Haverstraw through Bogota, Teaneck, and Bergenfield. It ceased operating as a train station in the 1950s and was converted to office use. Its simple, classically derived design is delicately detailed, as befits its small scale. Though it suffers from ill-conceived alterations to windows, doors, and roofing material, its

proportions are strong enough to mitigate these errors. Of particular note is the broad cornice, marked by a plain parapet, dentils, and a shouldered backing at the entry pediment. The brickwork is precise, including Roman arches at the window openings and diaper patterns flanking the original entry. Though the entrance has been made a window, the refinement of the detailing is evident on close inspection.

On August 26, 1971, Governor William Cahill created the New Jersey Sports and Exposition Authority for the express purpose of developing a new venue for horse racing and a home for the peripatetic New York Giants. What emerged from this endeavor says a lot about New Jersey culture in the late twentieth century. Love it or hate it, the Meadowlands remained one of the state's most controversial pieces of real estate for forty years. It is first and foremost a transportation hub, now marked by a new multiplatform station that receives thousands of motorists and commuters every day despite its swampy locale. More important, it has served as a coliseum for modern gladiators. In October 1976, Giants Stadium opened to a capacity crowd of 76,000 for a game with the Dallas Cowboys. Then the largest stadium of its type in the country, it begat many imitators that were built in exurban environments to take advantage of ready access to highways, thus removing sports from the dense urban communities that had traditionally supported them. The Giants, Nets, Jets, and Devils have prospered on suburban patronage since then, but many teams are moving back into cities to follow a new demographic. Awaiting demolition following construction of an even larger facility, the Meadowlands today is a symbol of sprawl at the center of the country's most densely populated megalopolis. In ten years this "shopping mall" for sports may become a large, vacant mall surrounded by asphalt, a monument to fossil fuels.

13

White Manna is one of the most intact landmark diners in New Jersey.
Located on River Street in Hackensack since 1946, it has all of the
architectural characteristics that one would expect in original diner
construction, namely, the streamlined metal and glass elements that give it
the appearance of a railroad car. Designed by architect Arthur E. Sieber, this
structure has an exterior wainscot consisting of repetitive metal panels with
a Gothic, pointed arch design. Above the wainscot is a continuous band of
windows supported by metal framing. Over the windows, slatted awnings
deflect rainwater. Glass block, ubiquitous in diners of this era, provides
rounded corners. The building is capped by a decorative, bellcast metal roof.
Two neon signs complete the composition: a banner sign along the edge of
the roof, and a free-standing sign on posts. White Manna is still a popular
regional meeting place despite competition from chain restaurants.

A patent for a ferry route between Weehawken and Manhattan was first
granted in 1700 by Richard Coote, governor of New York. The ferry was a
row and sail service, which was later superseded by steamboats at this site
and in nearby Hoboken. The route provided 259 years of continuous service,
until the last ferry left Weehawken in 1959. The new ferry terminal, designed
by the firm of Gruzen Samton of New York, opened in 2006 at the foot of
Pershing Street. Built on new concrete piers, the terminal is sheathed in large
metal panels with glass walls on the east and west. The glass pavilion on the
east gives access to boarding piers in the Hudson River. The light and airy
façades of the terminal are a welcoming gesture to commuters taking the
ferry to Manhattan and back. In 2009 the terminal was instrumental in the
rescue of passengers from US Airways Flight 1549, which made an
emergency landing in the Hudson River after both engines failed due to bird
strikes.

Hamilton Park, Weehawken

Hamilton Park in Weehawken enjoys one of the most beautiful natural settings and has one of the most impressive views of any urban park in the United States. Located at the top of the New Jersey Palisades, it is oriented to the east, overlooking the Hudson River and the skyscrapers of midtown Manhattan. The shape of the park is long and narrow and follows the cliff road almost the length of Weehawken north of the entrance to the Lincoln Tunnel. The park was built on the site of the duel between Alexander Hamilton and Aaron Burr in 1804, where Hamilton was mortally wounded. The duel killed one of the first proponents of a national banking system for the United States and the developer of the industrial city of Paterson. The event also quashed any aspirations that Burr may have had for higher political office, including the presidency. The park has been recently renovated with new installations of artwork and a paved promenade that gives improved access to its incredible scenic views.

The Hoboken Terminal is the hub for commuter trains, bus lines, light rail, subway lines, and ferry traffic. Constructed in 1907, it remains vital in the lives of more than 50,000 people who use its various systems daily. Designed by Kenneth M. Murchison, the terminal is most notable for the way in which it achieves architectural mastery both in its function of accommodating multiple means of transportation and in its aesthetic expression. Its waiting room, designed in the American idiom of the Beaux Arts style, is a masterpiece of public interior architecture. Organized symmetrically, it focuses on a monumental staircase and is dominated by a skylit ceiling of Tiffany glass, which is framed by a decorative cove and beams. The room is ringed by tall windows framed with pilasters, and its terrazzo floor echoes the ceiling's geometry. The terminal building is listed on the State and National Registers of Historic Places.

Today one of metropolitan New York's most popular tourist attractions, Ellis Island offers an example of how preservation can revive the fortunes of neglected places while also bringing history to life. During the 1890s, the small island near Hoboken was expanded to become the first official immigration station constructed by the U.S. government. After a disastrous fire in 1897, the firm of Boring and Tilton won a competition to design facilities that would handle the thousands of European immigrants who were arriving daily to pursue the American dream. The stately main building, with its four copper cupolas, remained in operation until 1954, serving also as a hospital and later a detention center for alien enemies arriving in America. After years of neglect, the island was opened to visitors in 1976, and in 1984 the main building underwent extensive renovation. Since 1990, it has been the home of the American Immigration Museum and Wall of Honor, where more than 20 million Americans have come to look for ancestors and gain an appreciation for what immigrants endured in order to attain citizenship in the United States. In 1998 New Jersey regained jurisdiction over a portion of the island created by landfill, leaving New York with the 3.5-acre museum site. Plans are under way to restore the remaining buildings for historical interpretation and tourism.

Although its legal location is in the State of New York, the Statue of Liberty sits close to the New Jersey shore in New York Harbor and is accessible by ferry from Liberty State Park. New Jersey shares a sense of ownership due to the statue's proximity and its embodiment of the values of liberty and freedom. A gift from the government of France to mark the centennial of the signing of the U.S. Declaration of Independence, the Statue of Liberty was not unveiled and dedicated until October 28, 1886. Frédéric Auguste Bartholdi was the French sculptor who designed and fabricated the statue with a small army of metal craftsmen. It is constructed of copper installed on a framework of metal bars, which are in turn attached to steel structural supports.

The supporting structure was designed by French structural engineer Gustav Eiffel, and the American architect Richard Morris Hunt designed its granite and concrete base. Located within the perimeter of historic Fort Wood, first built in 1811, the statue faces south toward the Atlantic Ocean and has welcomed generations of immigrants to our country. The statue underwent a major restoration in 1984 and was rededicated on July 3, 1986.

Liberty Science Center, Jersey City

Liberty Science Center is a nonprofit museum offering exhibitions and other learning experiences related to the sciences. It is a major architectural landmark in Liberty State Park, which is located on a New York Harbor site created from a former industrial area next to Ellis Island and the Statue of Liberty. Originally designed by Hillier Architecture, it has a significant, recent addition by Ewing Cole that provided a new entrance, welcome center, and exhibition galleries. The original building is similar to a streamlined basilica, with a tall central tower marking the original entrance. It has a concrete base with exposed aggregate to give the appearance of granite and is sheathed with a wall system of shiny metal panels. The nine rooms housing permanent exhibitions in the body of the building are terminated by a large domical structure that contains the largest IMAX theater in the United States. The addition is a refined structure constructed principally of glass but articulated with metal panels that unite it with the original structure. The addition appears to be a high-bay pavilion with a massive, trussed exterior balcony on the front and a continuous clerestory of glass on the side providing light to the interior. It also has a projecting entrance pavilion sheathed in glass, which affords enclosed access to the permanent exhibition galleries. Liberty Science Center is a destination for thousands of school-children and adults who take advantage of its hands-on science exhibits and special programs.

One of the state's most popular tourist destinations, Liberty State Park was
created from waterfront areas originally associated with rail transportation.
The Central Railroad of New Jersey (CRRNJ), chartered in 1849, connected
Manhattan ferries with the coal and iron of Pennsylvania via Phillipsburg.
The success of the ferry-rail connection in Jersey City drove CRRNJ to
construct a new "headhouse" terminal in 1889, allowing as many as 50,000
people a day to pass through the station on their way to and from Manhattan
by the turn of the century. The grand building, designed by Boston's Peabody
and Stearns, could accommodate 128 ferry runs and 300 trains per day,
using the twenty-track Bush train shed. When operations ceased and the
railroad went bankrupt in 1967, preservationists lobbied for adaptive reuse
of the site and placed the building on the State and National Registers of
Historic Places. Once the site was cleaned up around the terminal, the state
made plans to create a park on the open land. Governor Brendan Byrne
opened the park on June 14, 1976, to celebrate the nation's Bicentennial.
In 1985 Michael Graves designed a nature center for the wetland areas along
the river, and in 1989 the terminal building was rededicated following a
restoration. Of 1,212 total acres, 300 are currently open to the public.

The site of the Jersey City Medical Center on Montgomery Street at Baldwin Avenue has been continuously occupied by a municipal hospital for more than a century. From plain masonry and frame buildings to the steel, brick, and glass Art Deco skyscrapers of Mayor Frank ("I am the Law") Hague's day, the hospital expanded until it eventually outgrew Hudson County's needs. The Margaret Hague Maternity Hospital, designed by architect John T. Rowland, was built in 1929. It was the world's largest maternity hospital, and by 1939 it handled more than 5,000 births annually, more by several hundred than any other hospital in the continental United States. The complex is sited on

a prominence, an extension of the New Jersey Palisades, which affords a broad prospect of Manhattan. It consists of ten major high-rise buildings and a number of lower facilities. The combination of building heights and prominent siting makes the Medical Center one of the most important visual landmarks in Jersey City, and it serves as a point of orientation for its New Jersey surroundings. The complex is currently being converted into high-rise condominiums.

The Goldman Sachs Tower, completed in 2004, is the tallest building in New Jersey. It has been described as the most beautiful of New Jersey's skyscrapers, perhaps because the competition is not stiff. It is part of a cluster of tall buildings that seems emotionally more connected to Manhattan than Jersey City, and in this sense the tower may be seen as more anomaly than monument, rightfully belonging to neither bank of the Hudson. The building's architect, Cesar Pelli, is renowned for being able to elevate the design of the mundane and banal office building to a far higher level than most of his peers. The Goldman Sachs Tower is graceful and elegant, but its scale dwarfs its surroundings to such a great degree that it is unkind. It is a spectacular example of the inability of one good project to make a city, confirming that every good place is a series of small, thoughtful events instead of a single, grandiose statement.

23

William J. Brennan Courthouse, Jersey City

The Hudson County Courthouse was constructed in 1910, at the height of
Jersey City's power as a trade and manufacturing center. Like the nearby
Essex County Courthouse in Newark, the building is an elegant classical
structure decorated with murals and sculpture by some of America's finest
Beaux Arts–trained artists. Unlike its Newark rival, it is the work of an
architect of minor stature, Jersey City's own Hugh Roberts. Roberts received
the commission as a result of good old-fashioned nepotism: he was the
brother-in-law of Hudson County prosecutor William D. Edwards and New
Jersey governor and senator Edward I. Edwards. The building is sumptuous
and expensively decorated with overbearing marble, bronze, and limestone
ornament on the exterior. The interior is more graceful, featuring decoration
by Francis Millet and murals by Howard Pyle, Edwin Blashfield, Kenyon Cox,
and Charles Yardley Turner. Closed for a time in the 1980s, the building
came to symbolize not justice but patronage politics in one of the state's
centers of "pay to play" government. It was placed on the State and National
Registers of Historic Places in 1970, a move that probably saved it from
demolition when the county needed more modern accommodations. Today it
serves its original purpose and has been restored to its period grandeur.

Carnegie Library, Bayonne

As of 1920, New Jersey had thirty-five Carnegie libraries, approximately ten per million residents. The Bayonne Public Library is one of the most beautiful in the state, featuring a street-front colonnade that admits visitors to a forecourt. This Beaux Arts conceit was common in France, but it is unusual in an American context. The library is also unusual in its construction history. The original building, at the back of the site, was completed at a cost of $50,000 in 1903. The Carnegie Library foundation funded an expansion in 1913 at a cost of $30,000. A third construction

campaign occurred in 1930, at a cost of $300,000. The classical details of the original structure were maintained in the subsequent additions, but in each succeeding campaign the architects added more elegant, and more modern, touches. The architect of the 1903 building was Edward L. Tilton (1861–1933) of Boring and Tilton (designers of the main buildings at Ellis Island). The later additions were the work of Charles Shilowitz.

The Essex County Courthouse, designed by Cass Gilbert, is a masterpiece of American classical architecture and one of New Jersey's finest public buildings. It exemplifies the ideals of Beaux Arts classicism and the City Beautiful movement. The building's prominence is emphasized by its location on a hillside overlooking the downtown commercial area, its monumental staircase, the public gathering space below it, and the bronze likeness of the seated Lincoln by the sculptor Gutzon Borglum, who carved Mount Rushmore. The courthouse is conceived as a complete artistic creation from its columned exterior to its grand public spaces, lavishly detailed courtrooms, and interior finishes and furniture, all designed by the architect. The atrium is capped by stained glass domes by the Tiffany studios and contains flying staircases and four elaborate pendentive murals by Edwin Blashfield signifying Knowledge, Power, Truth, and Justice. Other courtrooms are graced with murals by Kenyon Cox, Francis O'Conner, and C. Y. Turner. The building's restoration was completed in 2005 by Ford Farewell Mills and Gatsch Architects.

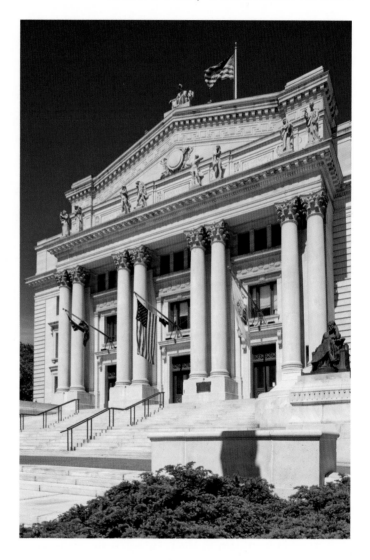

Gutzon Borglum's statue of Newark's heroes stands in the center of historic Military Park, the triangular "common" that was set aside by Connecticut Puritans when they laid out the city in 1668. The first map of the city called the area "The Training Place," perhaps indicating its intended purpose as a drill site for troops. Security was an issue when Newark was founded by settlers from New Haven shortly after the British captured New Netherland from the Dutch in 1664. Robert Treat, the leader of the original wave of 350 pioneers, first consulted on a site with Philip Carteret, the royal governor in Elizabethtown, who recommended the broad plains of the Passaic leading into what is now called Newark Bay. Broad Street, still the city's main thoroughfare, was laid out to run west from the banks of the river toward the Watchung Mountains. Military Park lies at the street's eastern edge, near the spot where Treat and his party came ashore in the winter of 1666 to begin their adventure in New Jersey.

Downtown Newark suffered much during the thirty years between the
infamous riots in 1968 after the assassination of Dr. Martin Luther King Jr. and
the completion of the NJPAC in 1997. But when the visionary arts entrepreneur
Lawrence Goldman opened the doors to his dream facility, silencing legions of
naysayers, Newark took a giant step forward. Now the sixth largest arts and
cultural center in the nation, the NJPAC has spurred a major revitalization
along the Passaic River and brought thousands of new music, theater, and
ballet patrons to the city. The architect, Barton Myers of Los Angeles,
described his building as a "celebration of people, community, and urban life."
The large gateway at the center of the façade makes an inviting gesture toward
Military Park and Broad Street. Inside, patrons get spectacular views of
skyscrapers, the riverbank, and the entire Newark metropolis stretching south
toward the airport. The main concert venue, Prudential Hall, has been called
one of the best in the world for its acoustics and sparkling interior. The
adjacent theater serves as a space for more intimate performances, including
plays and ballets. The building also has rooms for dining, parties, and small
conferences. It has become the cultural hub of a city that is becoming hip
again, recalling years in the early twentieth century when jazz clubs,
speakeasies, and vaudeville theaters lit up Broad Street every Saturday night.

The Newark Airport Administration Building is arguably the most significant aviation building in the country because of its relationship to the historic development of air transportation. Built in the Art Moderne style, it was at the time of its construction a revolutionary building type. Its requirements included passenger ticketing and waiting, baggage handling, weather monitoring, and air traffic control. As reported in the *Newark Evening News* on the occasion of its dedication by Amelia Earhart in May 1935, "the building has an average width of 50 feet, its front extends 200 feet, and its two wings of 100 feet each slope at 45 degree angles. This will enable eight transport planes to taxi to it at one time." The building is constructed of brick with aluminum and glass strip windows. The design included a glass and steel control tower, the first of its kind, to guide planes by a light signal system. The Port Authority of New York and New Jersey recognized the building's significance and recently moved, restored, and expanded it with a carefully designed addition to house airport administration, police, and air rescue and firefighting. The distinctive and historic features, such as the inlaid marble terrazzo floor, decorative plasterwork, metal ornament, and the air traffic control cab, were restored as part of the project.

Built during the final decades of the Pennsylvania Railroad's domination of Northeast passenger service, Newark's Penn Station was a product of engineering innovation as well as architectural creativity. In order to bring three tracks over the Passaic River, a massive 230-foot hinged bridge was constructed—the largest in the world at the time. Moreover, the Newark city subway required an underground extension to reach the new rail terminus. The complex was dedicated in March 1935 and has served the city proudly ever since. Though hemmed in by the working-class Ironbound neighborhood, the station is full of glorious ornament befitting the Streamlined Moderne era in American art. The architect was Lawrence Grant White, son of Stanford White, who became a partner in his father's firm in 1920. The classical touches are reminiscent of McKim, Mead and White's turn-of-the-century buildings, but the overall character of the spaces is Art Moderne.

On the north side of Newark, in what was historically a vibrant Italian American neighborhood, stands the magnificent Cathedral Basilica of the Sacred Heart, its two towers visible for miles around. Unlike New York City's still unfinished Cathedral Church of Saint John the Divine, this church was completed between 1899 and 1954 in a single building campaign, funded entirely by contributions from the Roman Catholic immigrants who labored in the factories and businesses that made the city prosper during the early twentieth century. One of architect Jeremiah O'Rourke's brilliant conceits in this design was the diagonal orientation of the two towers, which not only gives the exterior dynamic spatial qualities, but also links the cathedral to the downtown area to the southeast. The interior is based on French Gothic cathedrals, an unusual influence in Roman Catholic churches built mainly for Italian, Polish, and Irish parishioners.

The 359-acre park on the northwest side of Newark was originally called
Reservoir Park in reference to a large circular pool at its south end. Designed
originally as part of the Essex County park system by Barrett and Bogart, the
expanded landscape was redesigned in 1901 by Olmsted Brothers, successor
to Frederick Law Olmsted, the father of American landscape architecture.
Like Prospect Park in Brooklyn, Branch Brook contains a serpentine loop
road, a central lake, wooded rambles, and open meadows. In addition to
these Olmstedian features, the park boasts its own "Cherry Blossomland,"
a stand of more than 2,000 flowering cherry trees that were donated in 1927
by the Bamberger family of department store fame. The Ballantine gates,
designed by Carrère and Hastings, link the park with historic North Ward
neighborhoods. H. Van Buren Magonigle's 1914 Administration Building is
also a landmark within the park grounds. Branch Brook is one of Newark's
best-known institutions and has its own Friends organization, which
contributes needed financial and volunteer support for restoration and
improvement projects.

The Newark Museum is the state's largest public museum and a leader in education and the arts. It owes its existence and many of its unique collections to John Cotton Dana (1865–1929), the iconoclastic city librarian who convinced the city that it ought to have an art museum. His request was met with some resistance before officials finally, in 1903, allowed him to display American art on the library's upper floor. In 1909 Dana founded the Newark Museum Association, establishing science and children's museums as part of an omnibus program to give all Newark residents the chance to better themselves through learning. The original museum collections were displayed in the 1901 library on Washington Street, but Dana had plans for a new building under way following the end of World War I. The elegant Washington Street building designed by Jarvis Hunt was completed in 1926. That structure, at the right in the photograph, proved adequate to house expanding collections until 1982, when Michael Graves and Associates designed a major expansion that connected the building at the left with the historic Ballantine House (to the right of the photograph, not visible). The Graves design is one of the nation's first integrated attempts to create a new facility through the careful adaptive reuse of multiple historic buildings. Graves, an AIA gold medalist, considers the museum to be one of his best works, and many critics agree.

The first public library in Newark was established in 1888 and housed in the former Park Theater building. Librarian Frank Hill expanded lending and introduced open stacks where readers could browse for books. By 1897 the library was in need of more space, and a site was chosen at the eastern edge of Washington Park. Rankin and Kellogg, a noted Philadelphia architectural firm, designed the new granite and marble library in the form of an Italian Renaissance palazzo. The large central staircase ascends into a "cortile," or courtyard, covered with a glass skylight. When completed in 1901, the building had state-of-the-art collections and reading facilities. Like the New York Public Library, it maintained reading rooms on the top floors, allowing readers to request books from the lower-level closed stacks. When the fashion changed to favor open stacks, the large reading areas were retrofitted. Beloved by citizens, the library is always crowded with readers of all ages. Today it not only serves as a lending library, but also holds a noted collection of fine art prints and houses the New Jersey History Collection founded by the late Charles Cummings.

The building known today as Newark Symphony Hall was built in 1925 as the Salaam Temple of the Shriners, a Masonic order that flourished during the early twentieth century. Masons often bestowed extravagant funds and attention on their "mosques" or "temples," and this building was no exception, as the interior is decorated in gold leaf with a mélange of Egyptian and Greek ornament. The Griffith Music Foundation took over the management of the building in 1938, maintaining a schedule of vaudeville and concert performances by such luminaries as Arturo Toscanini, Lily Pons, and George Gershwin. As the city fell on hard times following the 1960s, the building lost some of its luster, but remained the home of the New Jersey Symphony Orchestra and other companies until the late 1980s. With the construction of the New Jersey Performing Arts Center, Symphony Hall became an alternate venue for Newark events, and it remains a vital part of the city's performing arts scene.

Ludwig Mies van der Rohe (1886–1969) was a dominant figure in twentieth-century architecture, both in the United States and abroad. His disciplined grids of steel and glass elements created models for corporate modernism that have persisted to this day. Although most of the canonical American buildings designed by Mies are in Chicago, where the architect lived and taught for the last three decades of his life, two can be found in Newark: the Colonnade and the Pavilion apartment towers. Built in 1959 on the north side of town, overlooking University Heights and High Street, the towers utilized the same curtain-wall vocabulary as the famous Lake Shore Drive apartments of 1949–1951 overlooking Lake Michigan. Though designed for the upper-income market, the Newark buildings suffered the fate of many fine structures in the Branch Brook Park area. As demographics changed and lower-income groups moved into the neighborhood, rents dropped and maintenance languished. Nevertheless, the buildings have aged well and continue to provide commodious housing at reasonable prices—and some of the best views in the city.

The handsome Gothic Revival building that serves as the alumni center for the New Jersey Institute of Technology was built in 1857. One of the oldest educational buildings in the city, it was originally the Newark Orphans Asylum. During the mid-nineteenth century, New Jersey was a leader in the provision of social services for indigent, mentally ill, or disadvantaged citizens. Like Greystone, the state asylum in Morris Plains, the orphans' asylum was built to raise children in a sympathetic, humane setting. The architect of the original building was John Welch. Cody Eckert designed the adaptive reuse when the New Jersey Institute of Technology elected to convert the building into offices during the 1980s.

This four-story building with an envelope of brick, steel, and glass is the flagship facility for the University Heights Science Park urban redevelopment project. The facility, designed by CUH2A and completed in 2002, contains three major research organizations: the UMDNJ Medical School's National Tuberculosis Center, UMDNJ Medical School's Department of Microbiology and Molecular Genetics, and the new Public Health Research Institute. The areas with brick façades contain laboratories for the various departments, the public and shared spaces are sheathed with glass, and the ground level contains an entrance lobby, auditorium, and service corridor. The complex is organized essentially as two separate wings that are oriented on an acute angle to each other, which creates a forecourt that guides visitors into the structure. A projecting glass element to the left of the entrance features an open stair, which serves as a "beacon" to the exterior entry plaza. A glass atrium links the two wings and gives access to public spaces on all floors. Although this building is a container for laboratories of high-tech research, its transparent lower levels maintain a human scale and connection to its urban neighborhood.

From 1883 to 1919, Andrew Carnegie provided grants for the construction of 1,689 libraries across the United States, 35 of them in New Jersey. As happened in communities across the country, Belleville's library was initially established by volunteers, the Tuesday Afternoon Reading Club, in a storefront. Carnegie's gift to the town of $20,000 ensured the construction of a new library, located at the corner of Washington Avenue and Academy Street. The architect, Charles Granville Jones, was a prominent local citizen who designed the Belleville town hall and the high school, among several other buildings. The original library building, erected in 1911, has, to our great misfortune, been obscured by an insensitive and ungainly addition. In contrast, when repairs necessitated that the interior be refurbished in the 1990s, the library board had the good sense to return to the character of the original. Expressing the classical underpinnings of the original design, the newly designated Carnegie Room, with its high-beamed ceilings, arched transom doorways, and decorative detailing, reminds us that the classical tradition is an ever-evolving and fluid one.

In Kearny, as in countless communities across the country, the public library
is considered by many citizens to be the heart and soul of the town.
Kearny's first lending library was located in the house of a prominent
resident in 1895. Later, the library was moved to the Freeman Building, on
Midland Avenue, which also housed the post office and local newspaper. In
1904 voters overwhelmingly approved the establishment of a free public
library, and soon thereafter Andrew Carnegie committed to provide $25,000
for the construction of a new building for it. The architect was Davis,
McGrath, and Kiessling of New York City. Completed in 1907, the building
is a Neoclassical masonry structure, arranged as a bilaterally symmetrical
rectangle, with two large reading rooms flanking the central circulation
space. The exterior treatment is straightforward, featuring a pedimented
entrance with Greek Doric columns in antis. The architectural detailing is
reserved to the point of meager, but the clear, strong plan and the direct,
no-frills expression accurately reflect the community that first erected it and
that now lovingly uses and maintains this bulwark of local social aspiration
and order.

Hoffmann–La Roche Building One, Nutley

The Hoffmann–La Roche buildings in Nutley form a national center for the study of oncology and inflammatory disease biology. Building One, completed in 1996, is a sophisticated modernist response to an office program. The design, by Hillier Architecture, is spare and assertive and consists of precast concrete façade panels, repetitive windows, and metal spandrel panels that break down the scale of the building. The entrance lobby and vertical circulation spine are marked by a projecting, butterfly-shaped glass element that rises the full height of the seven-story structure. Among its sophisticated features is its reliance on daylight to illuminate the workspace. The manicured grass lawn that meets the base of the building creates an abstract quality to this design composition in its suburban setting. The building's materials and articulation lend elegance to this deceptively simple structure. The monumental façades reflect the importance of the pharmaceutical research industry to the state of New Jersey.

The Edison Factory and Museum in West Orange is a National Historic Landmark operated by the National Park Service and one of the most culturally significant sites in New Jersey. The core buildings were opened in 1887 by Thomas Alva Edison, who had already invented the electric light bulb and the phonograph. Edison had moved from Menlo Park, New Jersey, to find space for expansion and manufacturing of his discoveries. Although the West Orange site was called the "Invention Factory," Edison did more than merely invent there. He developed better phonograph players and tested and manufactured them; he worked on X-rays, produced storage batteries, attempted to synchronize sound with moving pictures, and promoted the use of cement for concrete houses. He worked here until his death on October 18, 1931, at age eighty-four. The entrance to the West Orange site is through a brick arch next to a small frame gatehouse with decorative, beveled shingles. To the south of the arch is the main four-story laboratory building, Building 5, which contains Edison's research library and office, machine shop, materials storage, multiple work rooms, and laboratories. The building is classical in style, with Romanesque brick arches filled by windows between brick pilasters. The courtyard of the complex contains separate laboratories for chemistry and physics, a frame shed for experiments, and the "Black Maria," which was a covered studio for creating moving pictures. Much of the creative media expansion that now encircles the globe started here.

It is fitting that America's greatest inventor of mass-produced technology should reside in a house designed by Henry Hudson Holly, one of America's most successful purveyors of mail-order house plans. Glenmont is a handsome Queen Anne house in Llewellyn Park, thought to be America's first planned residential community. Edison purchased the house in 1886 and adapted it for his blended family when he moved his "Invention Factory" to West Orange. Constructed in 1880–1882 for Henry C. Pedder, an executive with the Arnold Constable department stores, Glenmont sat empty and completely furnished following the revelation that Pedder had built it with embezzled funds. Shortly after purchasing the estate, Edison married Mina Miller, the daughter of Lewis Miller, a prominent Methodist businessman and co-founder of the Chautauqua movement. Thereafter the house became associated with Edison's second family, much to the chagrin of the children from his troubled first marriage. A notorious workaholic, Edison spent relatively little time there even during the last decades of his long life, often falling asleep at his desk at the factory. Glenmont is now a part of the Edison National Historic Site operated by the National Park Service.

The wealthy drug merchant Llewellyn Haskell and the architect Alexander Jackson Davis (1803–1892) planned the picturesque "garden suburb" of Llewellyn Park between 1852 and 1854, while Haskell and eight partners were assembling about four hundred acres of forested land on the south side of West Orange, overlooking Newark and Manhattan. Haskell's stated aim was to provide "a retreat for man to exercise his rights and privileges," though his religious ideals suggested that residents might eventually find a new Eden in the community. Sites for country "villas and cottages" were arranged in serpentine loops around a central "ramble" planned for walks and nature watching. Considered now to be America's first planned community, Llewellyn Park retains its gated exclusivity, many of its villas, and a few areas of original landscape elements, such as the stone gatehouse that protects its residents from the outside world. Unfortunately, the public is invited in only when visiting Thomas Edison's mansion, Glenmont, so few Garden State residents know about the garden in their midst.

Stuart Richardson House, Glen Ridge

Frank Lloyd Wright is known as one of the most prolific architects this country has ever produced. He is widely revered by architects and just plain folks. His masterpieces are justifiably well known, and although much of his later work is mediocre, the little-known Usonian houses of his late career have had a profound impact upon the design and construction of the American single-family house since the 1950s. *Usonian* was Wright's term for an all-encompassing master plan for the American landscape. Through it, he hoped to house the middle class in individual houses designed to be generous in spirit and modest in size. These houses were built without basements, attics, or garages, and with flat roofs, small kitchens and bedrooms, and extensive expanses of glass doors to permit access to the outside. The Stuart Richardson House, designed in 1941 but not built until 1951, is an example of a Usonian house. The floor plan is based on a large equilateral triangle, which then has triangles and hexagons of various sizes superimposed. Their alignments are shifted and sides are omitted, creating a complex relationship of interlocking forms. A small kitchen forms one corner of a large triangle, while the living room with adjacent dining space encompasses the remaining spaces. The other two corners are masonry and contain inglenooks, one for a fireplace, the other for a small study. The wood ceiling, laid out in an overlapping pattern of cypress planks to reinforce the floor plan's geometry, is a wonderful and dynamic interior feature.

New Jersey was home to many larger-than-life industrialists who helped build America's economy during the early twentieth century. William Henry Nichols (1852–1930) was one of America's leaders in the chemical, dye, and metal industries. At one time he owned companies that produced sulfuric acid, ammonia, copper, and aniline dyes. He was also a founding member of the American Chemical Society in 1876, an organization that awards a medal in his honor each year. Nichols created the first modern chemical conglomerate by merging twelve smaller companies to form General Chemical Corporation in 1899. In 1920 Nichols joined with his sons Charles and William to form Allied Chemical and Dye Corporation from a conglomerate of disparate entities. Today the company is part of Honeywell, located in nearby Florham Park. The Nichols family began assembling a forty-acre parcel in West Orange as a country retreat in 1912. "The Farm," as they called it, expanded during the 1920s, when Charles Nichols hired Augustus Allen to create a French provincial "chateau" and garden. Today, the elaborate fantasy that Charles and his wife enjoyed is a popular restaurant and wedding venue.

Montclair's downtown, running roughly east–west along Bloomfield Avenue, is a vibrant, eclectic mélange of people, architecture, and activities. The range of expression is suggested, though certainly not completely captured, by the two building included in this book: the Clairidge Cinema and the Montclair Art Museum. The Clairidge, designed by William E. Lehman, opened in 1923 as a movie palace. Unlike many theaters of its day, it did not include a balcony. It did, however, feature an orchestra pit and dressing rooms. In the 1960s it was converted to a Cinerama theater. Sometime later it was divided into a triplex and, ultimately, a six-plex. Evidence suggests that the original majestic interior is largely intact behind the "black box" divisions inserted into it.

The Montclair Art Museum was established in 1914. Architect Albert R. Ross designed a classical brick and stone structure for it on the west end of Bloomfield Avenue, overlooking downtown Montclair and New York City. Ross worked for McKim, Mead and White, and was responsible on his own for a number of Carnegie libraries, including that for Atlantic City. The museum entrance on the west façade is a shallow, recessed two-story porch beneath four Ionic columns. Flanking the porch are pedimented gables, the blank elevations enlivened with fluted Doric pilasters and framed niches. The stately yet modest exterior is proof that scarcely windowed buildings can, in the proper hands, be handsomely designed. The museum is notable for its collection of twenty-one paintings by George Inness (1825–1894), whose work is prominently displayed in a room devoted solely to him. The museum's Native American holdings are also noteworthy, comprising more than 5,000 objects of art. With its active and successful Yard School of Art, the museum is constantly alive with activity. The building was doubled in size in 2001 under the direction of the architectural firm Beyer Blinder Belle of New York.

In 1902 Frederick Ellsworth Kip and his wife, Charlotte, planned the building of "Kypsburg." The mansion and the carriage house are unique examples of romantic, medieval-revival architecture, dramatically sited to recall another time and place. The stone gates, retaining walls, serpentine drives, and gardens add to the composition, uniting it with the rugged site while allowing the natural character of the ridge to prevail. The massive, semi-circular tower to the southeast is the most prominent feature of the structure, which is surrounded by a glazed veranda. The house is basically a two-story structure with crenellated parapets and a four-story tower. The interior woodwork is of English quarter-sawn oak. The front hallway has stained glass windows and contains a large stone fireplace. Eight monumental windows in the master bedroom suite look toward the New York City skyline. The third floor has a domical guestroom with a painting of a peacock above its fireplace. The building and grounds were recently acquired by Essex County for use as a park facility to assure its preservation.

The first county park system in the United States, Essex County's 6,000-acre greensward still ranks as one of the best in the nation. Planning began in 1895, and in 1898 the county had the foresight to hire the Olmsted Brothers firm to create a model system of large and small parks tailored to neighborhood needs in its increasingly populous towns. The nephew and son of Frederick Law Olmsted continued the ideals of the founder of American landscape architecture in their park planning during the early twentieth century, designing some of the most important public landscapes in America. New Jersey is fortunate to have some of their masterpieces in Essex County, such as the beautiful Verona Park, a space that gives pleasure to thousands of visitors each year.

The largest percentage of New Jersey's significant Jewish population
emigrated from Eastern and Central Europe during the late nineteenth
and early twentieth centuries. The oldest congregations, however, came
to Newark following the German upheavals of 1848. Such was the case
with the founders of B'nai Jeshurun, one of the largest temples in the city
by 1960, when an exodus began toward Newark's western suburbs.
Leaving its splendid Neoclassical temple behind, the congregation first
constructed a modern facility in South Orange before building the present
synagogue in 1968. Gruzen and Partners, a leading New York firm, designed
the imposing prow-shaped sanctuary, placing the Ark at the apex, below a
dramatic vertical stained glass window. Now one of the most vital Reform
congregations in the state, B'nai Jeshurun is one of many temples that had
their origins in Newark's historically Jewish neighborhoods. Most of their
rich history would be forgotten but for the wonderful fiction of Philip Roth,
who continues to make it a central theme in his work.

The fourteen-room Georgian plantation house at the core of the building we call Liberty Hall was built by William Livingston in 1772 and remained in his extended family until 1995. As such, it is one of the oldest continuously inhabited houses in America and contains voluminous records and artifacts of the Livingston-Kean family. Governor William Livingston (1723–1790), the first to serve the state of New Jersey after the Revolution, was a member of the first and second Continental Congresses and a delegate to the Constitutional Convention. After his daughter married into the Kean family, the clan maintained a high social and political profile: congressmen, senators, state representatives, and military leaders resided on the estate for two centuries. The house received many alterations through the generations, most significantly in the mid-nineteenth century by Colonel John Kean (1852–1914). The Kean family created a museum on the twenty-three-acre estate in the late 1970s, maintaining an endowment for the care of the buildings. The museum recently became part of nearby Kean University in Union, which will continue its interpretation as a historic house while adding a study center to the grounds.

As the responsibilities of school districts have expanded in recent decades, the need for adequate facilities specifically for disabled students has become clearer. This school was designed to accommodate 144 severely, multiply disabled students ages three through twenty-one. The educational program is comprehensive, including a component devoted to occupational, speech, and physical therapies. In addition to specialized preschool programs, the school offers a career center in which students perform tasks similar to those found in communities, in order to help transition students into the workplace upon graduation. The school, designed by Rothe Johnson in 1981, contains 45,000 square feet on one level and features minimal and clear circulation patterns. Classrooms are arranged around common lobbies to minimize corridors. Natural light is brought into the interior via extensive clerestory windows. Courtyards along the circulation path amplify the amount of daylight and further connect the interior to the exterior. The result is a series of spaces that are open and welcoming.

Steuben House, River Edge

The Steuben House in River Edge is a fine example of what is called New Jersey "Dutch" architecture. There are many extant examples of the style east of the line that divided East and West Jersey in the eighteenth century. This house was first built in 1752 by Jan Zabriskie and expanded in 1767. It faces the Hackensack River in a settlement called New Bridge Landing, where George Washington's troops crossed on their retreat through New Jersey from New York and the Battle of Long Island (Battle of Brooklyn). The crossing was a hotbed of activity during the Revolutionary War, and several skirmishes were fought here. The house is a large, rectangular structure built of coursed brownstone ashlar. Its one-and-one-half stories are capped by a gambrel roof with a swept profile characteristic of Dutch colonial houses. On the front of the building, the flare extends to cover a broad porch supported by nine slender Doric columns over the entire length of the façade. The upper gables beneath the gambrel roof are faced with brick. Given to Baron von Steuben at the end of the Revolution for his contributions to the war effort, the house is now owned by the state of New Jersey and is the major component of New Bridge Landing Park. It also serves as the museum headquarters of the Bergen County Historical Society.

As one of the nation's leading industrial states, New Jersey was the site of many pioneering advances in engineering during the nineteenth century, including the development of water systems serving major cities in the state and region. One of the most significant was constructed in Bergen County, already one of the most populous areas of New Jersey in the late nineteenth century. In 1881 the Hackensack Water Company received its charter and purchased the site of several old mills near the center of Oradell. Creating a reservoir, the company constructed the first of its pumping stations shortly thereafter. By 1911 the handsome group of brick buildings we see today was complete, housing early steam-powered pumps and other hydraulic systems. During the 1920s George Spalding, a company engineer, developed the first carbon filtration system for water purification, still the standard for water quality throughout the world today. When the company closed the site in 1990, the historic buildings were threatened with demolition. A broad coalition of local and state groups saved the site in 2002, and today a nonprofit group is raising funds for the restoration of the buildings and landscape.

The Rose Center is the former residence of James Rose (1913–1991), a
noted landscape architect and theorist who became one of the leaders in the
modern movement in American landscape architecture. After practicing in
New York City, first with another firm and then on his own, Rose eventually
abandoned large-scale work to concentrate on the design and construction
of private gardens. Chief among Rose's interests was celebrating the
interpenetration of interior and exterior spaces. He also believed that the
rapidly changing world around us directly affects how we live, and he
focused much of his attention upon designing spaces that were flexible
enough to be adapted as changing needs dictated. In 1953 Rose began
building the house he first envisioned while stationed in Okinawa, Japan,
in 1943. His fascination with the properties of overlapping spaces can be
traced to this time. The house is a constructed example of his belief in
the interrelationship of interior and exterior, and of the exchange between
public and private spaces. He devoted himself to building what he designed,
allowing him the opportunity to improvise in situ. His other work is
concentrated near his home in northern New Jersey. His former house is
now a landscape research and design study center, and a shining example
of the ideas he pursued so enthusiastically.

The Carmel Retreat Center began in 1905 as the summer residence of Clarence Chapman, a wealthy New York businessman. Located on approximately 350 acres in the Ramapo River Valley, the house became a year-round home in 1910. The design was inspired by traditional country houses of the Hudson River Valley, with large boulders as an expression of that connection. At its heart, the house is a straightforward, rectangular mass anchored at each end by bold stone chimneys. Its roofline is notable for its shed dormers, emphasizing the sheltering aspect of the roof.

Over the years, the house grew, as befits a country estate, with the addition of a carriage house, greenhouse, and additional outbuildings. The Chapmans, however, were forced to sell everything in the Great Depression.

Since 1954 the house has served as a retreat center for the Carmelite order. It underwent an extensive renovation beginning in 1988 and continues to serve the region as a center for retreats, reflection, and education.

Skylands Manor, Ringwood

Now the centerpiece of the New Jersey State Botanical Garden, Skylands Manor was built by the noted financier and horticulturalist Clarence McKenzie Lewis, beginning in 1924. The site was chosen for its spectacular views—to the north, the Ramapo Mountains and New York's Hudson River Valley; to the south, the lakes and forests of the upper Passaic watershed. Lewis hired John Russell Pope (1874–1937) to design a sprawling Tudor house and the noted landscape firm of Vitale and Geiffert to create gardens and farm plots that would rival any in the United States. When fully planted and mature during the 1930s, the landscape was undoubtedly New Jersey's most extensive and beautiful example of what many consider the golden age of American garden design. Restoration of the gardens and main house continues to be a challenge, as state funding for historic buildings and parks has not kept pace with the needs of this important landmark.

New Jersey is the home of America's first planned "town for the motor age,"
Radburn, in the Bergen County town of Fair Lawn. The accompanying
photograph does not show the sweeping greensward that is Radburn's
trademark, but rather a less heralded but more important feature. Henry
Wright and Clarence Stein designed Radburn to segregate pedestrian and
automobile circulation in order to foster community among residents.
Moreover, multifamily housing clusters were grouped in modified cul-de-sacs
in order to maintain a parklike atmosphere throughout the three
neighborhoods, each circumscribed in a half-mile radius to allow for easy
walking between shopping and residences. Indeed, in order to create an
uninterrupted park in the center of each "superblock," the designers created
underpasses like this one. Designed in 1928, the three neighborhoods in
Radburn were largely completed by 1930. The failing economy put an end to
the dream of a truly pedestrian-centered new town at Radburn, and nothing
built since has come close to replicating its serene, bucolic environment.
Today's developers are about as aware of Radburn's significance as the
average Bergen County resident is of its presence near the chaotic
intersection of Routes 4 and 17. Sadly, the positive lessons concerning
community planning learned at Radburn and adapted at century's end by the
Congress for New Urbanism, led by architects Andrés Duany and Elizabeth
Plater-Zyberk, have had virtually no impact upon New Jersey development.

Lambert Castle, Paterson

Since many of Paterson's silk mills are now gone or badly renovated, the most important symbol of its heyday as the silk capital of America is Lambert Castle, just southwest of the city center. The building can be seen from Interstate 80, looming impressively from the sandstone cliffs of Garret Mountain. Catholina Lambert (1834–1923) came to America from England at the age of seventeen to make his fortune in textiles and was immediately successful. Beginning as a bookkeeper in a Boston cotton mill, the young man worked his way up to become a partner in his own firm, Dexter, Lambert and Company, at the age of twenty-three. Moving to New York to join the growing silk trade, he bought several mills in nearby Paterson to expand his business. Once among the "captains of industry" who were building elaborate residences on large estates, Lambert decided to erect his own showplace on land he had acquired in 1891. Completed by the end of 1892, the "castle" was intended to evoke the craggy keeps of Yorkshire, where Lambert spent his boyhood. Its rather ungainly proportions and chunky details indicate that the patron had a hand in its design, perhaps shoving aside the architect (unknown today) to get the desired effect in sandstone, granite, and wrought iron. Before he was done, the silk king had installed an art gallery (1896, demolished), an Italian garden, and an observation tower (1900, restored). Today the castle serves as a museum and the headquarters of the Passaic County Historical Society, which restored the building in 2000.

The Paterson Museum is housed in the former erecting shop of the Rogers
Locomotive Works, one of America's industrial giants during the nineteenth
century. The site was once a bustling factory complex of more than a dozen
buildings that were constructed to take advantage of the hydropower from
the upper raceway of Paterson's Society for Establishing Useful Manufactures
(S.U.M.) canal system near the Great Falls. The first buildings were
constructed in 1831 for the production of textiles, Paterson's early
commercial engine. The Rogers Locomotive Company acquired the site
in 1854 and built machine shops, an administration building, and other
factory structures until 1879. Rogers was one of the country's most
innovative companies, leading the world in the production of steam
locomotives for decades. Among its achievements were the introduction of
the counterbalanced driving wheel (1837), the hollow spoke driving wheel
(1839), expansion brakes (c. 1840), and the link motion system (1849).
The Historic American Engineering Record documented the five remaining
buildings in the Rogers complex as part of the Great Falls S.U.M. National
Historic Landmark District in 1973.

Paterson's first public library, housed in the mansion of Charles Danforth, one of the city's leading industrialists, was destroyed in the fire of 1902. Danforth's daughter, Mary Danforth Ryle (1833–1904), donated the funds for the new Danforth Memorial Library, which was built at a cost of $225,000. The wife of William Ryle, the largest silk importer in the United States, Mary Ryle was Paterson's leading philanthropist and a beloved civic leader in what was then America's silk manufacturing capital. Opened in May 1905, the library featured an open-stack reading room, children's library, art library, auditorium, and a collection of 30,000 volumes, one of the finest of its kind in the United States. The elegant limestone structure joined a group of superb Beaux Arts classical public buildings that included City Hall (Carrère and Hastings, 1899) and the domed Passaic County Courthouse. The architect, Henry Bacon Jr. (1866–1924) of the firm Brite and Bacon, was a protégé of Charles F. McKim and later designed the Lincoln Memorial in Washington, D.C. (1912–1922). The library design is reminiscent of Bacon's masterpiece in Washington—a frieze of wreaths and names of great writers wraps the entire building below the simple cornice. The interior planning is masterly as well, in the best tradition of Beaux Arts design "by the axes," in the words of John Harbeson. Bacon's affinity for classical antiquity (his brother was an amateur archaeologist in Greece) shows in the details, such as the bronze torchères flanking the entrance. This unheralded gem, like much of Paterson's architecture, deserves to be better known.

The sandstone ruins of this historic mill date to the earliest days of manufacturing in Paterson. Once the system of canals began to supply power to lots in the district controlled by the Society for the Establishment of Useful Manufactures, merchants began to build mills such as this one, originally constructed in 1813 as a rolling mill and nail factory. The Patent Arms Manufacturing Company purchased the lot in 1836, tore down the existing buildings, and built a 100-by-40-foot sandstone factory there. Here John and Samuel Colt produced their first classic revolvers. Gun production was short-lived in this location, however. By the 1840s the buildings were part of an expanding textile industry focused on silk fabric. The mill operated until the late twentieth century, when a fire destroyed the beautiful loft building and its spire, long a symbol of Paterson's industrial prowess. According to a nineteenth-century account, "On the spire which surmounted the bell tower was a vane very elaborately made in the design of a finished gun, and in front of the mill was a fence, each picket being a wooden gun, and the whole was beautifully painted." Sandstone from the ruin was collected after the fire and remains stored on the site for future use in consolidating and interpreting the structure.

The "Great Falls" of the Passaic River at Paterson is one of America's natural
wonders. During the first century of the new Republic, thousands of tourists
flocked to see water spill over the gorge near the center of the new
industrial town that was a brainchild of Alexander Hamilton. Still the largest
waterfall by volume south of Niagara on the eastern seaboard, the site is
now surrounded by a city that has seen better days. Attempts at reviving
the area around the falls have met with little success through the years.
In 1976 President Gerald R. Ford visited Paterson and declared the Great
Falls Society for Establishing Useful Manufactures (S.U.M.) area a National
Historic Landmark. In 2004 Governor James McGreevey created Great Falls
State Park to preserve the riverbanks around the historic millraces.
Paterson's poverty and a series of insensitive and unrealized redevelopment
plans contributed to the area's decline during the 1990s. Fires ravaged many
of the historic mill buildings in the district at this time. In 2001 a group
of concerned citizens successfully sued the City of Paterson to stop an
ill-advised development scheme close to the falls. The preservationists
won another victory in 2009, as the U.S. government, under the National
Park Service, allocated $1.6 million for archaeology, environmental
remediation, and site stabilization for the precious S.U.M. district. Recently
the state commissioned a master plan from James Corner to create a new
environmental park around the falls, a step that gives further hope for a
future to match the glorious past.

Dey Mansion, Wayne

This finely detailed Georgian house was built between 1740 and 1750 by
Dirck Dey, a Dutch-born planter, and completed by his son Theunis.
Theunis was commander of the Bergen County Militia and offered his home
to General George Washington during the Revolutionary War. Washington
used it as his headquarters in July, October, and November 1780. The house
is built of brick, with brownstone belt courses, corner quoins, and window
surrounds. It is two-and-one-half stories tall, with a high attic capped by a
gambrel roof. Two large parlors in front and two smaller rooms in the back
flank the wide central stair hall, which runs from the front to the back of the
house. In its framing and masonry construction, the house reflects both
Dutch and English influences, as well as urban and rural styles, rare for
mid-eighteenth-century homes in the area.

The Fanwood Railroad Station is one of the earliest extant railroad stations in New Jersey, built in the 1870s as part of the Central New Jersey Railroad. It is a long and narrow structure, about 16 feet wide and 55 feet long, with a plan that was typical for New Jersey railroad stations of the period, such as those at Matawan, Hopewell, and Pennington. The building originally contained two waiting rooms, one for men and one for women, separated by a stationmaster's office and ticket room. The second and third floors were likely used for residential purposes by railroad personnel. While many stations of the period were constructed of masonry, this one is wood framed and has elaborate Gothic Revival details. Its jerkinhead, pitched roof is pierced by Gothic dormers and trimmed with a carved, quatrefoil woodwork at the eaves between turned drops at the corners. The perimeter of the building is protected by a broad overhanging canopy roof, with a decorative belt course above it. Restored in phases by the Borough of Fanwood in the 1990s, the old station now has a new life as a community center.

The stately sandstone building known as "Old Queens" was built between 1809 and 1825 to the designs of John McComb Jr. (1763–1853), the New York City architect responsible for the historic city hall in lower Manhattan. As the main building of Queens College, the Federal-style structure served several purposes: classroom building, college chapel, faculty offices, seminary, and faculty dormitory. In 1825 Colonel Henry Rutgers, a Revolutionary War hero, gave the college $5,000 and a bell to be rung during class hours. The bell was installed in a cupola donated by Stephen Van Rensselaer, another New York philanthropist, and is still in place today. In 1976 the building and its surrounding campus were designated as a National Historic Landmark.

The Daniel S. Schanck Observatory on the Old Queens campus at Rutgers is an octagonal brick and sandstone structure designed to evoke the Temple of the Winds in Athens. *The Antiquities of Athens,* by James "Athenian" Stuart and Nicholas Revett, first published in 1762, had become a popular source in the United States for those seeking to design in a Greek Revival manner, and it is the likely inspiration for the Schanck Observatory. This prototype, chosen by architect Willard Smith, was a perfect form for an astronomy laboratory to be used by the Rutgers Scientific School. The building was dedicated on June 18, 1866. When functioning, it included a revolving roof to protect telescopes and a laboratory wing at the rear for faculty and students. It is part of the National Historic Landmark Old Queens campus in New Brunswick.

Standing adjacent to the Rutgers campus in New Brunswick, this handsome Gothic Revival church is the work of Patrick C. Keely (1816–1896), the most prolific designer of Catholic churches in America. Keely emigrated from County Tipperary, Ireland, to Brooklyn in 1842, setting up in business as a builder, his father's trade. His first major work was the church of Saints Peter and Paul in Williamsburg, dedicated in 1846. Thereafter he became the preferred architect for parishes throughout the United States and Canada, erecting some seven hundred churches. The vast majority of his designs were English Gothic, though he planned a massive cathedral in Brooklyn along French models that was never finished. The cornerstone of Saint Peter's in New Brunswick was laid in 1856, but the building was not completed until 1865 due to the Civil War's strain on the economy.

Like many mid-nineteenth-century churches in New Jersey, the building was constructed with local brownstone, a material that has not weathered well in an atmosphere filled with automobile pollutants. Keely also designed large parish churches in Paterson, Jersey City, and Hoboken.

The Johnson & Johnson World Headquarters building in New Brunswick is one of the most prominent urban landmarks in central New Jersey. Designed by the office of internationally known architect I. M. Pei (b. 1917), the complex represents the commitment of this corporate giant to remain in its original, urban location as part of the city's redevelopment. The company had the option of relocating to a suburban campus, but chose instead to lead the renewal of the City of New Brunswick. The concept for the complex was a city in a park and a park within the city. The design solution is one that acknowledges its context with a combination of mid-rise pavilions that are scaled to the surrounding architecture of Rutgers University and of Johnson & Johnson's earlier Colonial Revival buildings. The fifteen-story office tower that is located on the commercial side of the complex is in scale with other downtown buildings in New Brunswick. The architectural language is modernist, consisting of flat and curved metal panels and International-style strip windows. The light color palette of the buildings forms an attractive contrast to its carefully landscaped campus, designed by Hanna/Olin, which is a visual amenity for the downtown area.

the Casino, Asbury Park   PSK G

2
The Shore Region

The region from Sandy Hook south to the end of Long Beach Island stretches down some of the state's most attractive beaches and popular coastal communities. From Sandy Hook to Asbury Park to Beach Haven, the region possesses many desirable destinations, all within easy driving distance from the rest of the state. Island Beach State Park offers the longest protected stretch of oceanfront in the state. Interestingly, the Shore Region spreads inland as far as Englishtown, indicating how strong the pull of the ocean is upon the population's psyche. The architecture and urban pattern of this region are low-scaled and patchwork. Distinct downtowns, like Spring Lake, and neighborhoods exist, but they have been enmeshed within seemingly scattered roadways and the one-dimensional roadside construction that typifies this type of development. Towns have lost their edges in this area's expanding web. Fittingly, however, the area has a cohesive identity, and its residents are proud of their patch of turf within it. This may be the quintessential region of New Jersey, as it is reached and linked by the venerable Garden State Parkway, in a state for which the road is iconic. It is difficult to define a single place as its cultural, demographic, industrial, or emotional center. Rather, the focus is eastward and extends linearly north to south, to encompass the ocean and the bay, where fishing, swimming, boating, clamming, and hanging out are the primary activities. These simple pleasures are why people stay—and why visitors come back year after year.

Fort Hancock, Sandy Hook

Aptly named, Sandy Hook is a narrow sandbar at the northern end of the Jersey Shore that extends into New York Harbor. It is part of the Gateway National Recreation Area, which spreads across the metropolitan area watersides. The geography of Sandy Hook made the site ideal for military facilities intended to protect the harbor, and it has housed fortifications of some sort since the American Revolution. Battery Potter was constructed there for coastal defense in 1893. Both of its twelve-inch guns could fire a thousand-pound projectile as far as seven miles. The following year four twelve-inch mortars were installed in a concrete battery connected by tunnels. The community of Fort Hancock was laid out on the west side of the spit facing the bay in 1895, but the land was not cleared and the first buildings were not completed until 1899. Planning for the new community was done by Captain Arthur Murray. After obtaining design advice from his architect friends John Carrère and Thomas Hastings, Murray developed drawings depicting structures in a Colonial Revival style. The most notable aspect of Murray's design is the positioning of the officers' housing, which has unobstructed views facing the bay, with the parade ground at the rear. Barracks for enlisted men are arranged in an arc on the eastern edge of the parade ground, forming a vast enclosed space for drilling, practice, and ceremonies. The fort remained active into the Cold War as the home of one of the Nike missile sites ringing New York City. It was deactivated in 1974 and turned over to the National Park Service.

This charming structure dates from 1864 and was designed by Richard Mitchell Upjohn (1828–1903), son of the founder and first president of the American Institute of Architects. Upjohn Sr. was a key figure in introducing the Gothic Revival in the United States and also designed Saint Mary's Episcopal Church in Burlington. The basic vocabulary for All Saints' comes from the elder architect's book of designs for rural churches, *Upjohn's Rural Architecture* (1852), which influenced builders throughout the United States. In the Navesink church the "carpenter" details of the gables and bell tower contrast with the local sandstone used for the walls. The younger Upjohn was very active in New Jersey, designing half a dozen other Episcopal churches, including Saint John's in Dover, another National Register property. His largest and most notable building is the Connecticut State Capitol in Hartford (1873–1880), the only statehouse built in the High Victorian Gothic style.

Twin Lights Lighthouse, Highlands

New Jersey's long coastline was once safeguarded by dozens of lighthouses guiding ships into New York Harbor on the north or the Delaware Bay on the south shore. Twin Lights, located in Highlands, stood at the mouth of the Navesink River, inland from Sandy Hook. The first two lighthouses on the hilltop, constructed in 1828, were made of wood. Why were two lights constructed? Ship captains needed to distinguish these beacons from the single light at the tip of Sandy Hook. Joseph Lederle designed the imposing sandstone building, which consists of square and octagonal light towers, crenellated, linking hyphens, and a central keeper's house, and he supervised its construction in 1862. The site was host to a number of signal events: the first Fresnel prisms used in America (1841), the first electrified light station in the country (1898) with its own generating plant, and the first demonstration broadcast of Marconi's wireless telegraph (1899). The lighthouse was decommissioned in 1949 and is now a state historic site open to visitors.

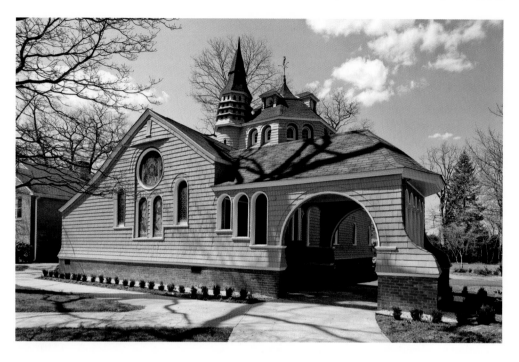

Rumson is fortunate to have this Shingle Style gem, recently restored by
Farewell Mills Gatsch Architects. The design, featuring a unique wooded
dome and cupola, is the earliest extant work of Thomas S. Hastings
(1869–1929), whose firm designed the New York Public Library in Manhattan.
Hastings's father, a noted Presbyterian minister in New York, served as
summer pastor in the village, called Oceanic at that time. In 1885 he asked
his son, then a draftsman with McKim, Mead and White, to design a new
chapel for the small but wealthy congregation of "cottagers." During the
1880s this area of the Jersey Shore was a playground for America's elite, and
elaborate summer houses were being built from Middletown to Long Branch.
Just as the church was finished in 1886, Hastings left Stanford White's office
to form a partnership with John Merven Carrère and to compete against his
old firm for many of the plum domestic commissions associated with New
York society families. Among Carrère and Hastings's nearby houses were
"Firenze" (1900, for Daniel Guggenheim), "Norwood Park" (1905, for Murry
Guggenheim), and a smaller summer residence for S. W. Glazier (1903), all in
Elberon. The Hastings family continued to maintain a summer residence in
Rumson following the turn of the century, but this church is the only
remnant of their sojourns.

The Bluffs is a development of twenty townhomes on the waterfront in Red Bank, which incorporates three existing residences. Located on Front Street, the project was completed in 1989 and is locally renowned for being a celebration of the town's ubiquitous Victorian architecture. The focal point of The Bluffs is the Hubbard House, a Second Empire house erected in 1868. Immediately adjacent are a Queen Anne house and a nineteenth-century vernacular house sporting multiple alterations. The architect of The Bluffs, Jerome Morley Larson Sr., sought to create an enclave protected from the street and open to magnificent views to the water. His solution was to add four identical structures to the site, each with three units canted from the central axis. A swimming pool, a public waterfront walk, and private docks complete the connection to the water.

The recession that began in 1987 affected Red Bank significantly, especially its retail enterprises. With the establishment of a Special Improvement District in 1991, the town began a resurgence. A well-known presence on Broad Street is the Count Basie Theatre, originally known as the Carlton Theatre. One of the most significant works of William Lehman, a prolific Newark-based architect, the Carlton was constructed in 1926 as the State Theatre, and that name is still inscribed in terra-cotta above the theater's ornate marquee. A product of the Golden Age of Hollywood, the theater was designed to showcase both live performances and moving pictures. The façade contains several storefronts that were leased to help support the operations of the theater. From the entrance, guests proceed through a ramped outer lobby to the inner lobby, which is articulated with two monumental staircases (one at each end), decorative plaster and painting, and an oculus in the ceiling that provides a visual connection to a mezzanine floor level. The theater seats about 1,500 guests and is lavishly decorated with cast and molded plaster ornament, a domical ceiling, and a proscenium with sculptural relief that includes cherubs and dragons. In 1984, shortly after the death of William (Count) Basie, the theater was renamed in honor of the Red Bank native. The theater was recently restored by Farewell Mills Gatsch Architects with new chandeliers and sconces, decorative painting, and a new "atmospheric" mural of a blue sky with clouds on the dome.

Bell Labs, Holmdel

Completed in 1962 and expanded in the following two decades, Bell Laboratories was designed by Eero Saarinen, America's foremost architect of the 1950s and 1960s, with a planned landscape by Sasaki, Walker and Associates. It is a massive, modernist landmark of international significance, not only for its architectural integrity and the importance of its designers, but also for the many contributions to communications technology made within its walls. With additions by Roche-Dinkeloo, Saarinen's successors, the complex grew to nearly 2 million square feet by the 1980s. The building has a six-story, mirror glass façade and is composed of four major building blocks connected by a cavernous glass atrium with sky bridges. Innovative interlocking wall sections in the laboratories were designed to be blast resistant. At its peak, the building provided workspace for more than 6,000 researchers and other employees. It functioned as an independent city with internal support services on its suburban campus. The spare, glass envelope reflects its surroundings by day and serves as a lantern at night. A large water tower, resembling an oversized transistor, marks the entrance to the campus. The building is currently vacant, and redevelopment plans are being proposed.

Adaptive reuse of historic buildings has become a necessity in our increasingly energy-conscious world. When Monmouth University acquired the Murry Guggenheim estate in 1960 as a donation from the widow of its owner, the home was converted into a library. The college had previously refurbished Shadow Lawn, the Hubert Parson house (1927, Horace Trumbauer, architect), as an administration building. To its credit, the college maintained the essential character of both buildings while expanding them for academic functions. The photograph shows the splendid garden façade of the Guggenheim house, with its semicircular belvederes (porches) designed by Carrère and Hastings in 1903. Completed in 1905, the house and gardens received a gold medal from the New York Chapter of the American Institute of Architects.

Quail Hill Boy Scout Camp in Manalapan Township, consisting of two hundred acres, is located close to the geographic center of the state. It was protected from development in 1992, when the town council sold development rights to the state. The All Faiths Chapel, designed by Jerome Morley Larson Sr., is located within the woodlands of the camp, tucked into a natural amphitheater. The surrounding trees, tall and spindly, are paralleled by the slender and spare design of the chapel, erected in 1968. The structure, approximately fifteen feet tall, consists of four curved, laminated beams joined to create a spire. A skirt of wood shingles connects the legs and provides a modicum of shelter. The effect is simple yet suggestive, implying the responsibility to intrude delicately upon the earth.

New Jersey has a history of utopian idealism dating back to the seventeenth century. One of the most interesting experiments in communal ownership of homes, factories, and farms occurred in 1933, at the height of the Great Depression. Benjamin Brown (1885–1939), a Ukrainian-Jewish immigrant in the poultry business, set up a commission for Jewish Farm Settlements under the National Industrial Recovery Act. Using a grant of $500,000, he purchased 1,200 acres of land in Monmouth County, calling the new venture "Jersey Homesteads." In 1935 the architect Alfred Kastner and his young assistant, Louis I. Kahn, designed houses, a factory, retail stores, and farm/market buildings in a simple International Style idiom, using concrete masonry units for wall systems. Construction of forty-two houses was complete by 1937, and a clothing factory opened that same year. A farm market supplied produce from cooperative agriculture. The factory soon failed, however, and the Farm Security Administration closed the agricultural cooperative in 1940. The federal government then sold the houses to the residents, who managed to maintain a sense of solidarity throughout the war years. After the war, the homesteads offered a haven for artists and intellectuals. The most famous of them, Ben Shahn, suggested that the town be named for Franklin D. Roosevelt and saw to it that a memorial was erected there in the president's honor. Roosevelt was placed on the National Register of Historic Places in 1983, and its buildings remain as a testament to the vision of Brown, Kastner, Shahn, and the other progressive Jews who dreamed of a working-class utopia amidst the Jersey meadows.

The Asbury Park Convention Hall, an exuberant brick and terra-cotta pleasure palace, consists of three elements: the Paramount Theatre, the Convention Hall, and the Arcade. The Arcade connects the other two structures and terminates the northern edge of the Boardwalk. The Casino Building anchors the southern end of the Boardwalk and served, when constructed, as a large amusement hall. Designed by Warren and Wetmore, who also designed Grand Central Station, the buildings were begun in 1929 and completed by July 1, 1930. They enjoyed only limited success due to the Great Depression and the outbreak of World War II. Both the Convention Hall and the Casino are

steel frame buildings with brick walls, terra-cotta and copper ornament, and copper-clad windows. The entrance to the Paramount Theatre is an elaborate arcade that faces an urban park to the west. The west wall of the theater has three monumental arches articulated with stone and terra-cotta. A brick and terra-cotta water tower, recently restored, rises above the theater and serves as a town landmark. The Arcade is a beautifully detailed public space with a glass curtain wall facing the Boardwalk and trimmed in copper. The Convention Hall has terra-cotta ornament and copper sculptural elements throughout. These details emphasize a marine theme, including ocean waves, shells, seahorses, and a magnificent three-masted ship atop the parapet. The Casino also has a copper and glass façade containing elaborate, pressed metal decoration. At the ends of the Casino's main façade are fluted, cast-stone piers capped by large copper lanterns. Although the Convention Hall has been renovated, the Casino is an architectural ruin awaiting full restoration and adaptive use.

Carousel House, Asbury Park

In the late 1800s, Asbury Park became one of the most famous resorts in the United States, offering beautiful beaches, a wide boardwalk, and major buildings for public amusement. The Carousel House was an important addition to the city's amusement building tradition. Built in the late 1920s as an appendage to the Casino Building, this one-story round structure was purpose-built for a carousel. The building consists of an exposed decorative steel structure with projecting brackets that support a broad roof overhang. It has a standing seam metal roof, with acroteria of alternating size at the roof edge. Arched openings exist between the radial structural supports and have swirled glass roundel windows within the arches. The conical roof is capped by a lantern and a copper dome edged with colored lights. Unfortunately, the historic carousel was dismantled and sold, but one can imagine its sights and sounds adding to the life of the Boardwalk. The structure is being restored, and it is hoped that the original carousel will be returned one day to Asbury Park.

This unprepossessing, one-story, flat-roofed building facing the ocean in Asbury Park is considered the unofficial performing home base of New Jersey's own Bruce Springsteen. Though never an advertised performer, Springsteen often joined the band and jammed onstage, frequently with Southside Johnny and the Asbury Jukes. By word of mouth and local radio promotion, the Stone Pony came to be known as the place on the Jersey Shore to hear rock 'n' roll. Performers who have graced, or prowled, its stage include Elvis Costello, Joan Jett, and Jon Bon Jovi. The club closed in 1998 after a foray into alternative rock, and then reopened in 2000. Although it continues to offer performances virtually every night, it has not regained the cachet that once made it famous as a destination. The club remains, however, a landmark on the Asbury Park beachfront as the home of the "Boss."

The centerpiece of the Christian community of Ocean Grove is the Great Auditorium. It was completed in 1894, built to replace earlier tabernacles that could no longer accommodate ever-growing crowds. The space was initially designed for 10,000 people; today, after the installation of new seating, the capacity is 6,200. The large, column-free auditorium space is created by iron trusses spanning the hall. These trusses bear on stone foundations, but the remainder of the hall is wood. The ceiling is vaulted and curved to enhance the acoustic properties of the hall, allowing preachers to be heard by the vast audience prior to amplification. The ceiling's varnished surface still reflects the light from incandescent bulbs in their original locations. Multiple doors flank the auditorium and, when opened along with windows and wood panels, provide cross ventilation. The room is a welcoming and enfolding space, simple and wholesome in its design and its finishes. On the exterior are fourteen tents, laid out in a pattern dating to 1869. The tents were initially intended as temporary shelter for the throngs of visitors who came to the camp meetings. In excess of 700,000 visitors arrived from New York City in 1877. A shed attached to the rear of each tent contains a kitchen and bathroom. These tents are rented for the summer months, but prospective tenants can wait ten years on a list before being able to rent one. The Auditorium now houses performances throughout the summer, secular as well as religious.

Ocean Grove was established in 1869, when the Ocean Grove Camp Meeting Association was formed by a group of Methodist clergymen. The camp meeting movement had begun in the 1700s in response to the absence of both houses of worship and ordained ministers in the vastness of the American frontier. Because travel was arduous and meetings were often distant, it was practical for attendees to camp at the meeting site. The movement became popular throughout the nineteenth century and still continues in some places. Ocean Grove's location on the shore between New York and Philadelphia offered an ideal spot, attractive and convenient to both cities. Meetings there immediately proved popular, and attendance grew spectacularly. To better accommodate the crowds, permanent structures began to be erected in the 1880s to replace the temporary shelters. The prevailing architectural style is reflected in the Victorian character of the village. Even the simplest buildings have highly ornate porches with carved and turned wooden ornament. Tourists soon joined meeting-goers, descending upon the small community in the millions, attracted by its religious events and by its oceanside location. Ocean Grove is a designated National Historic District. It is rightly honored as a planned community, its nineteenth-century character nearly intact and well maintained.

On the oceanfront, between Shrewsbury to the north and Sea Girt to the south, lies Spring Lake, a small gem of a community. Named after the natural springs that create the local lake, Spring Lake has the feel of a small town. Its streets run parallel and perpendicular to the shoreline, establishing a readily understood pattern for orienting oneself. Its compact main commercial street, Third Avenue, parallels the shore, running north from Devine Park. Housing in the town is predominantly Victorian in style, and street trees planted long ago create an iconographic sense of neighborhood. Its shoreline, two miles long, boasts the longest noncommercial stretch of boardwalk in the state. One of the local landmarks, the Sea Girt lighthouse, is actually located in Spring Lake. Now a museum, it was the last operating lighthouse residence in the country.

The imposing Essex and Sussex is the last of the resort hotels that once made Spring Lake a destination for vacationers in the New York metropolitan area. Constructed in 1914 to replace a smaller hotel, the building remained in operation as a hostelry until the 1970s. Several attempts to reuse it during the intervening years met with little success, until the Applied Development Group of Hoboken petitioned Spring Lake in the 1990s for the right to convert the building into condominiums for the elderly. Initially denied its zoning variance, the company sued and was granted its relief in 1997. Since then, construction has proceeded on the project, with a sales office offering 160 one-bedroom units at market rates. Much of the rehabilitation work was completed before the economic downturn starting in 2008 resulted in a cessation of work on the project.

Saint Catharine Church, Spring Lake

Saint Catharine Church was built by Martin Maloney, a Philadelphian who maintained a summer residence in Spring Lake, as a memorial to his daughter Catharine, who died of tuberculosis in 1900 at the age of seventeen. The architect was Horace Trumbauer (1868–1938), also of Philadelphia, who catered to the nouveau riche in his native city who were spurned by the old Quaker-Episcopalian oligarchy. The diminutive classical building is something of an oddity in the rustic seashore town of Spring Lake, but maintains its gravitas nonetheless. The cottagers who flocked to this charming resort came from Philadelphia, New York, and New Jersey in search of sea air and compatible society during the late nineteenth century. Less pretentious than Rumson or Deal, and a good deal more upscale than Atlantic City, Spring Lake has maintained its reputation as a quiet oasis on the shore catering to middle-class vacationers.

Jerseyana, the lore of the Garden State, has always included hoopla.
The Jersey Devil started things with a bang in 1735, and we've never looked
back. Nothing, however, compares to the extravagant claims made about the
Jersey Shore, a place that even early natives considered paradise. It was
claimed that President James Garfield, dying of an assassin's bullet, would
instantly recover if given a few days of sea air in Elberon. (He didn't.) In the
"Gay Nineties" Atlantic City's Boardwalk was rife with signs touting the
miraculous healing powers of elixirs and beauty creams. No Miss America
won her crown without using Pond's Cold Cream and Vanishing Cream.
The improbability of such extravagant boasts has not dampened the
enthusiasm of tourists, who still flock to the honky-tonk fortunetellers and
arcade swindlers on boardwalks from Asbury Park to Wildwood. Despite the
natural beauty of the Atlantic Ocean, people don't go "down the Shore" to
watch seagulls. They go to experience the ineffable joy of dizzying rides,
carousels, saltwater taffy, beer, and sunburn. The Shore may be Jersey's best
place of all, but don't believe what people tell you about it. Just go.

Designing a summer retreat near the Jersey Shore for George Jay Gould, the son of railroad tycoon Jay Gould, architect Bruce Price evoked the lavish houses of the Georgian period in England and Scotland, hence the name Georgian Court. The formal landscape elements, also designed by Price, included an Italian garden, a lagoon and sunken garden, and a Japanese garden. Sculptural ornamentation enhanced the landscape, and a wrought iron fence with distinctive terra-cotta entrance gates framed the property. Electric lights, "son et lumière," were installed to amplify the experience, one of the wonders of New Jersey in 1898. The estate was sold to the Sisters of Mercy in 1923 and converted to academic use. The mansion is constructed of materials indigenous to southern New Jersey: brick, sand-finished stucco, terra-cotta, and wood trim. Although the building at first glance appears to be one-and-one-half stories high, it is actually three stories. The port-cochère is supported by multiple Ionic columns, and the decorative wood trim of the balconies, windows, and doors is elaborately detailed. Beyond the main entrance, a double-height, vaulted space features a monumental marble staircase, an open second-floor balcony, and elaborate decorative plaster, painting, and sculpture on the walls and ceiling.

Built as a Works Progress Administration project in 1938 at the corner of Clifton and Main Streets in Lakewood, the post office designed by Noboru Kobayashi is a fine example of the Art Moderne style. It is a monumental structure of buff brick with terra-cotta trim of two types: architectural panels and moldings of tan color to resemble limestone; and massive, bright green and white decorative panels that form borders around the windows and doors. The green panels are also known as faience tile, which is often seen as decorative trim in seaside buildings in New Jersey. The tiles are highly ornate and molded with rosettes, swags, scrolls, and vines. The building sits on a raised platform and is reached by a flight of stone steps. The entrance is centered on the front façade and presents a glass door with sidelights and transom that are probably not original. The front façade contains large multipane windows having fifteen over fifteen lights. Two large bronze lanterns flank the entrance, and a gold relief sculpture of an eagle covers the window over the door. In case there is any doubt as to the use of this building, it has a broad and flat terra-cotta cornice with incised green letters that match the faience tiles.

One Airport Road, Lakewood

This professional office building was designed by Noboru Kobayashi.
The spare and elegant design is made up of pure geometric forms that recall
both Shinto temples and the Louis Kahn Bath House in Ewing Township.
The complex consists of nine square pavilions of ascending dimension offset
from each other on diagonal axes. The pavilions are capped with steeply
pitched, pyramidal roofs covered by wood shingles. The roofs are supported
on regularly spaced wood columns with large glass windows between them.
The windows sit on a solid plinth sheathed with flush board, horizontal
siding. The siding is pierced at regular intervals by wall-mounted HVAC units
that project slightly from the surface. The roofs have built-in gutters that
collect rainwater and direct it through scuppers into the reflecting ponds
from which the pavilions rise. The building is bordered by a landscaped
berm that encloses a manicured lawn on the sides and back of the site.
The U-shaped drive and parking area give access to a flagstone terrace,
which creates a quiet and enclosed entry sequence to the building.

Solar Village, a senior citizen housing project near Jackson, is an early example of multi-tenant buildings designed and constructed according to sustainable design principles by solar innovators Douglas Kelbaugh and Robert Lee. The housing seeks to be environmentally responsible and energy efficient by making use of various active and passive solar strategies to provide for the energy needs of the dwelling units. Tenants are accommodated economically in one- and one-and-one-half-story frame structures that are sheathed with wood shingles, are heavily insulated, and have double-glazed windows. The houses are oriented to face the same direction, taking maximum advantage of the southern exposure. The open front porches have roll screen roofs to provide shade in the summer and access to direct sunshine in the winter. This project from the early 1980s is both modest and friendly to its surroundings, and its solar design is considered progressive.

Saint Mary's Russian Orthodox Church, Jackson

Just prior to World War II a significant number of "White" Russians came to the United States, settling primarily in New York, San Francisco, and Chicago. Deeply religious and socially conservative, the immigrants organized a branch of the Russian Orthodox Church in America that had its headquarters in New York City, and they established a monastery in Jordanville, New York, to train clergy. One large colony of "old believers" left New York for Lakewood, New Jersey. They established Saint Vladimir's Orthodox cemetery in Jackson in 1939 and began building a chapel there in 1940, using the churches of late medieval Russia as design precedents. Saint Mary's Church was dedicated on February 25, 1952, by Metropolitan Leonty Turkevitch of New York. The congregation remains one of the most vital and active in the nation, with services held in Russian each Sunday. New Jersey has long been a host to religious minorities from all over the world. Nearby Lakewood has large communities of Hasidic Jews and Tibetan Buddhist monks, who worship in much the same way the Russians do, as largely separate cultures within the dominant Anglo-American society.

Lakehurst has long been the East Coast center for zeppelin, dirigible, and blimp aviation. It is the location of the most famous dirigible disaster in history, the destruction of the *Hindenburg* on May 6, 1937. The German dirigible exploded and burned while landing after a trans-Atlantic flight. Hangar One often housed two rigid airships at a time and also sheltered the *Hindenburg* when it was in the United States. Hangar One was built in 1920 by the Lord Construction Company to house the Navy airship *Shenandoah,* which was more than 600 feet long. The hangar was constructed out of ten long-span steel trusses that form an arched structure containing open, column-free space for airship storage. It was one of the largest interior spaces in the world when constructed: 966 feet long, 350 feet wide, and 225 feet high. The doors at the ends of the building each weigh 1,350 tons and stand 136 feet wide and 177 feet high. When Hangar One was constructed, it was said that it could house three Woolworth Buildings (the tallest skyscraper of its time) lying on their sides. The size, design, and use of this structure make it a unique landmark in the history of aviation.

Dillon's Creek Marina, Island Heights

The marina at Dillon's Creek in Island Heights was completed in 1987.
In addition to the piers and boat slips, the marina, designed by
Richard E. Martin, consists of a series of small buildings connected by
decks. The buildings are simple rectangular masses with pitched roofs.
Clad in a dark-stained clapboard, they recall myriad boating and waterfront
environments all along the Northeast coast. The architect's inspiration,
in fact, was the archetypal New England fishing village. The place is
commendable for its relaxed and comfortable atmosphere. Its sense of scale
is humane and unpretentious, befitting the leisure activities that are its
raison d'être.

Once known as the Barnegat Bay Decoy and Baymen's Museum, the Tuckerton Seaport has evolved into a maritime museum village. Located along historic Tuckerton Creek, the forty-acre site includes seventeen historic and re-created buildings connected by a boardwalk. It also includes a wetlands nature trail, two houseboats, a decoy gallery, an operating boatworks, a decoy carving workshop, and the re-created Tucker's Island Lighthouse. The lighthouse is a two-and-one-half-story frame structure with a tower, balcony, and octagonal glass cupola centered on the pitched roof. This is a typical arrangement for a lighthouse designed as part of a residential structure. Tuckerton Seaport is also home to the Jersey Shore Folklife Center, where the diverse communities and traditions of the Jersey Shore and Pinelands are researched, documented, and interpreted. The center presents folk art programs and exhibits, and celebrates the creative spirit of the region. Also at the Seaport, the Jacques Cousteau National Estuarine Research Reserve, managed by Rutgers University and housed in the Tuckerton Yacht Club, conducts scientific research, hosts educational programs, and serves as a steward for the resources of its unique setting.

Barrier Islands

New Jersey is fortunate to have a long Atlantic Ocean coastline, famously and fondly referred to as simply "The Shore." That Shore is largely made up of a string of barrier islands, almost all of which are developed, and all of which are certainly destinations. Landscape architect Ian McHarg studied this ecosystem, one of his first projects there, in 1965, in response to a significant hurricane. Not surprisingly, his sensible and logical recommendation that the barrier islands be abandoned, because they were subject to constant erosion, was ignored. Barrier islands are simply described as long, narrow strips of island paralleling the mainland shore. Generally separated by shallow bays, these islands are the result of sand deposited by waves and currents. They serve to protect against coastline erosion from surf and tidal surges. These islands, when unimpeded by human development, are in constant flux, generally moving in the direction of prevailing currents and wind. Long Beach Island has been moving closer toward the mainland shore, and the Barnegat Inlet has moved south about a mile over the past one hundred years. Island Beach State Park is New Jersey's best example of barrier island ecology in its natural state. It runs for ten miles and is home to a diverse population of wildlife, including ospreys and peregrine falcons, and vegetation that has changed little since Henry Hudson described the coast in 1609.

Starlux Wildwood
PSK-G

3

The Greater Atlantic City and Southern Shore Region

The broad and long beaches of the southern New Jersey shoreline have long been a principal attraction for the state's residents. The presence of such a long stretch of beach-lined coast in close proximity to the metropolitan centers of New York and Philadelphia made New Jersey's seaside towns logical holiday destinations.

The well-established road and rail links between New York and Philadelphia, Wilmington, Baltimore, and Washington ensured that the most populous lines of transportation bypassed Cape May. That neglect allowed the Victorian buildings erected in the town's heyday to remain unmolested by the pressures of so-called progress, saving the area to become an attractive, low-key resort. Of particular interest is the locale's fame as a birding site: Cape May is on the migratory path for hundreds of thousands of birds each year. The Cape May National Wildlife Refuge encompasses more than 8,000 acres set aside to protect the natural habitat.

Atlantic City became the stellar attraction of the New Jersey coast in the late nineteenth century, partly as a result of direct rail connections to the major cities, but also because it could boast of the nation's first boardwalk. Atlantic City quickly became a serious resort destination, and its hotels were among the grandest and most lavish in the land. The grandeur of its architecture gradually decayed until legalized gambling was envisioned as the region's savior in the 1970s. Although the casinos brought income back to the city, they also destroyed the old hotels, and the newer architecture does not deserve a second glance. It remains highly debatable that the urban center that spawned Monopoly has been much improved by gambling, let alone "saved."

The region is full of interesting sites, including the Doo Wop architecture of the Wildwoods. This is a collection of nearly sixty seaside motels and small commercial buildings featuring neon signage, curvy and wavy forms, and vivid, fantastic colors. The Wildwoods have become a mecca for mid-twentieth-century design aficionados, who relish visiting what may be the largest group of roadside architecture in the country.

The Delaware Bay shoreline consists of extensive mudflats and marshlands, providing excellent habitat for wildlife, but less attractive for human settlement. The larger towns along the bay are set well inland, like Bridgeton, which has the largest historic district of any city in New Jersey.

Although golf was not invented in New Jersey, many historic moments in the history of the game have occurred on courses in the Garden State. Baltusrol, Pine Valley, and Canoe Brook are famous with professionals, while many other courses attract an international clientele. Famed course architect Robert Trent Jones designed the three courses at the Seaview Marriott Resort in Galloway Township, including Troon, a seaside course recalling its Scottish namesake. The resort clubhouse, shown in the photograph, is a distinguished example of golf club architecture that complements the beauty of the Shore landscape.

Boardwalk Hall, Atlantic City

Once the largest building of its kind in the world, Atlantic City's former convention hall has been host to many historic events besides the Miss America Pageant for which it is famous. Perhaps most notable was the 1964 Democratic Party convention, when Lyndon Johnson and Hubert Humphrey were nominated amid protests from a disfranchised delegation from Mississippi. The massive steel frame building was designed by Boston's Lockwood, Greene and Company, an engineering firm, and dedicated on May 31, 1929. During World War II the hall became an Army Air Force training facility. From 1942 through 1945, nearly 400,000 soldiers passed through the building. The arched steel trusses that support the roof of the main hall remain an engineering marvel. The photograph shows the limestone-clad Boardwalk façade, once flanked by beautiful hotels and shops. Following the introduction of casino gambling in 1979, most of the Boardwalk's charming, exuberant architecture was replaced with vacuous corporate hotel designs that belong in the Nevada desert, not "by the beautiful sea." This building is a tangible reminder of the earlier period in Atlantic City's history.

Atlantic City's Carnegie Library was designed by Albert R. Ross, a local architect who won a competition sponsored by the city in 1902. It served as the public library from 1905 until 1985, when a new and larger facility was constructed on Atlantic and Tennessee Avenues. In addition to serving the public as a lending library, the old building was the home of art classes and became the repository of the Alfred M. Heston Collection of Atlantic City artifacts and records. That collection is now in the main library in the county building. The Carnegie Library has a handsome Classical Revival façade executed in terra-cotta. After a period of abandonment, it reopened as the Carnegie Library Center of Richard Stockton College of New Jersey. Today it houses university classes and public events.

Atlantic City was once home to dozens of zany tourist attractions, from Steele's Fudge Shop to the Diving Horse on Steel Pier. Most vanished between the downturn of the 1970s and the destructive 1980s, when casinos moved all the fantasy indoors to the private gaming rooms. The Knife & Fork Inn has somehow survived. The building was constructed in 1912 as an exclusive men's club, but soon ran into trouble for continuing to serve liquor during Prohibition. After having been closed down by the government, the club reopened in 1927 as a restaurant under the ownership of Milton and Evelyn Latz. Thereafter it became the most memorable eatery in the city, frequented by famous entertainers and many business and government celebrities. Located at the intersection of Atlantic, Pacific, and Albany Avenues on the north side of town, it was the place to meet and be seen during the heyday of the resort. In 1997 the family's sole heir, Mack Latz, sold the building to another longtime city restaurateur, Frank Dougherty, owner of Dock's Oyster House, who has restored its allure for new tourists.

The Senator Frank S. Farley State Marina in Atlantic City is a public facility
maintained under the auspices of the New Jersey Division of Parks and
Forestry. Located on Clam Creek, it sits across from the Trump Marina resort.
The facility can accommodate yachts up to 300 feet in length and has
640 floating slips. The marina offers the full range of services expected of a
first-class facility, and has the added benefit of immediate proximity to the
attractions of Atlantic City.

The Atlantic City Race Course was dedicated in 1946, the brainchild of a group of investors that included Bob Hope, Frank Sinatra, Sammy Kaye, and Xavier Cougat. The course was constructed by another investor, John B. Kelly, father of the late Princess Grace of Monaco. During the inaugural season, jockeys included Eddie Arcaro, Johnny Longden, and Ted Atkinson. Facilities at the track were among the most luxurious in the United States. The massive roof used technology employed in airplane hangars during World War II. The one-and-one-eighth-mile oval remained in full use until the mid-1990s, when competition from Philadelphia caused the owners to reduce racing to a few events per year. The fate of the course is in doubt as of 2010.

The photograph depicts nothing but a tragic vacancy on the vast Monopoly board that was Atlantic City. Following the 1979 legislation that brought gambling to America's first middle-class resort, the landmarks that gave the city its swagger and status as an entertainment capital vanished one by one. Once the most renowned of a dozen glittering piers along the Boardwalk, Steel Pier is now a concrete hulk covered with ephemeral amusements. The 1,780-foot-long "Showplace of the Nation" opened in 1898, sporting a concert auditorium that would soon become the most coveted venue for emerging talent in the United States. From the late 1920s until the mid-1960s, Steel Pier featured more stars than the Milky Way—Frank Sinatra, Dean Martin and Jerry Lewis, Milton Berle, Jackie Gleason, Glenn Miller and his Orchestra, Benny Goodman, Paul Whiteman, and Count Basie, to name but a few.

The picturesque Tudor city hall in Ventnor, the upscale suburb of Atlantic
City, reminds residents that their island was once the most elegant resort in
America. The building is the work of Vivian Smith (1886–1952), a talented
local architect who designed many of the best buildings in Atlantic and
Ocean Counties during a forty-year career. After studying architecture in
Philadelphia, Smith returned to New Jersey in 1914 to design a town hall for
Ocean City, where he had been born and raised. His Beaux Arts training
allowed him to design in any one of the popular styles of the early twentieth
century. The Segal Fruit, Real Estate & Law, and Guarantee Trust buildings in
Atlantic City followed, along with numerous churches, public buildings, and
residences. In 1928 he was hired to create a low-scale, residentially friendly
town hall for Ventnor, which wanted nothing of the monumentality of its
neighbor to the north. The building is one of the most charming of its type
in the state and presaged the idiom of many 1980s and 1990s civic
structures in the suburbs.

The metal monument that was erected to sell real estate at the end of Atlantic City's barrier island is today one of New Jersey's most recognizable symbols. "Lucy the Margate Elephant" was patented by James V. Lafferty in 1881 as one of a series of metal eye-catchers that were to be built up and down the eastern seaboard. Sixty-five feet from toe to howdah, she weighed ninety tons and was built of sheet metal on a wooden frame. Almost immediately, the salt air began to corrode her skin and rot her skeleton. She stood for nearly fifty years without repairs, until residents successfully petitioned to have her named to the National Register of Historic Places in 1966. Three restorations later, it appears that the problematic pachyderm will be here for another hundred years.

A grand Beaux Arts edifice may seem incongruous for an oceanfront town known as a resort destination, but Ocean City's City Hall celebrates city government with elegance. Built in 1914 according to the design of Atlantic City architect Vivian Smith (1886–1952), the structure is noted for its extensive terra-cotta detailing at cornice, entablature, and parapet. City Hall's three-story exterior was extensively restored in 1995 and 1996, and the building was listed on the National Register of Historic Places in 1997. It is a commanding presence, designed during the era of civic awareness known as the City Beautiful movement. On the principal elevation, shown in the photograph, the two upper floors are recessed and divided into seven bays, delineated by engaged columns. The central bay is framed by paired columns and contains the arched entrance, reached by monumental stairs from the street. The tawny-colored brick is rusticated at the building's base and corners, and the window surrounds and base are rendered in stone. The brick and stone work, coupled with the pale window trim color, give the building a bright and lively presence in contrast with its monumentality.

Boardwalks are almost literally a line in the sand. They are the demarcation between the untamable forces of nature and the often paltry structures we erect to provide ourselves shelter and amusement. They are obviously corridors of human traffic, but also gathering places. One can sit and gaze at the ocean or observe the passersby. Ocean City was originally developed as a Methodist resort, based on the successful model of Ocean Grove. Its boardwalk, first constructed in the 1880s, was accompanied by a string of oceanfront activities, including a music pavilion, which operated year-round. The original boardwalk was dismantled and stored during the off-seasons. After a fire destroyed it in 1927, it was replaced with one made of western fir and redwood, supported on a concrete structure of pilings and beams. A new "music pier" replaced the pavilion in 1929. Although no longer a Methodist resort, Ocean City is known as a family-friendly destination. Its boardwalk contains a happy assortment of shops, concessions, and amusements along its length. The mood generated by these establishments is upbeat, perhaps a bit goofy, but certainly fun. And on the eastern side of the boardwalk, just look at that beach.

Doo Wop Preservation: Caribbean Motel, Wildwood

Following the success of seaside resort hotels in Atlantic City, Asbury Park, and Spring Lake, beach communities began to proliferate on the Shore's southern barrier islands. Once highways were built in the 1950s linking Shore towns like Avalon, Stone Harbor, and Wildwood to Philadelphia, a new building type emerged to serve weekend tourists: the motel. Built cheaply and quickly with flat slab concrete systems, Jersey Shore motels became the architectural equivalent of muscle cars and string bikinis, often demonstrating more flair than their West Coast cousins. When these ebullient symbols of mid-twentieth-century style were threatened in the 1990s, residents of Wildwood joined with architect Steven Izenour (a co-author of the influential study *Learning from Las Vegas*) to create the Doo Wop Preservation League. Though Izenour died before preservation efforts were complete, his legacy lives on in restored motels like the Caribbean.

Frank Furness's jagged, whimsical house for Dr. Emlen Physick, built in
1878–1879 by contractor Charles Shaw, is quite literally the centerpiece
of Cape May's late twentieth-century economic revival. Home to the
Mid-Atlantic Center for the Arts and Humanities, the house and its grounds
become the locus of spring and summer tourism in this extraordinary
Victorian resort at the edge of the Delaware Bay. Before it was purchased by
the city in the 1970s, the building was threatened with demolition. Years of
patient fundraising and preservation have seen both the Physick House and
the entire town become a jewel of New Jersey heritage tourism. Though
Furness (1839–1912) was but one of many prominent Philadelphia architects
who designed cottages and hotels for late nineteenth-century summer
residents, his reputation as America's most eccentric architect of the period
gives this building a special cachet. Docents at the house delight in pointing
out the bizarre fireplace mantels and flamboyant carved woodwork in the
stair hall while relating events in the lives of the architect and patron. At
Christmas the house takes on an even more dramatic air, as rich Victorian
decorations festoon every room. The Physick House is quite likely the most
visited architectural landmark in the state outside of New York Harbor.

Cape May Inns

Once known as the queen of resort towns on the eastern seaboard, Cape May grew rapidly during the early nineteenth century as a result of ferry service down the Delaware River from Philadelphia. Seeking the "rest cure" of sea air and fleeing the filthy streets and foul air of the city, thousands of summer visitors were coming to Cape May by the early 1830s, after the construction of the first hotels on the island, including the Mansion House and Congress Hall. When regular rail service arrived in 1863, the town grew even further, but competition from larger resorts nearer New York kept the city from developing beyond the original island tracts. More significantly, Cape May was prone to fires. The first major blaze in 1856 destroyed the magnificent Mount Vernon Hotel, then the largest in the United States. Massive blazes in 1869 and 1878 nearly obliterated the town's tourist economy. The buildings that remained into the twentieth century were spared from demolition by economic doldrums until the 1970s, when a revival of interest in Victorian architecture sparked the extraordinary renaissance that saved these tourist cottages and turned them into bed-and-breakfast inns.

Congress Hall is the largest of the classic Cape May Victorian resort hotels to have survived into the twenty-first century. It is the third hotel to occupy the site; each was called the Congress. When the second hotel burned in the fire of 1878, the owners retained architect E. F. Meyer and builder Richard J. Dobbins to create a "fireproof" brick building. The design is reminiscent of the Marquis de Lafayette Hotel, which featured an L-shaped design lined with colonnades on the inner façades. Stephen Decatur Button designed the rear wing, paralleling the ocean, in 1880 and erected a music pavilion in the courtyard, which no longer stands. During the 1990s a consortium of local developers initiated a multiyear restoration of the building using federal tax credits for historic preservation. The ground floor contains shops and a restaurant. The result is a charming evocation of nineteenth-century resort life that will delight any tourist with an interest in history.

This picturesque lighthouse was designed by Alexander Parris (1780–1852), a Boston architect and student of Charles Bulfinch (1763–1844). Erected in 1849, the building is located within the Hertersville Refuge in Maurice River Township. Originally known as the Maurice River Lighthouse, it shares the same domestic form seen at many other lighthouses along the Jersey Shore. The building is essentially a five-bay, two-and-one-half-story brick house with a lower service wing. It has a corbelled brick cornice and a standing seam, pitched metal roof. Centrally located on the roof is an octagonal tower containing the light. A pedestal above the roof, sheathed in metal, supports a wood observation platform. The platform and guardrail surround a glass lantern containing the light, which has its own metal roof. The Maurice River Historical Society was formed in February 1971 with a goal of restoring the lighthouse. Just five months later, however, the lighthouse caught fire and burned. The society has since applied for historic preservation grants and has succeeded in restoring the shell and structure of the lighthouse, including its windows, doors, and shutters.

The Landis Theatre is one of the finest works of Art Moderne architecture in New Jersey. Designed by William Lee for Eugene Mori in 1938, it originally held 1,200 seats for movies and live performances. Lee, a Philadelphia architect, designed many theaters and public buildings in the Delaware Valley, including the Lansdowne and Sedgewick Theatres near Philadelphia and Mitten Memorial Hall at Temple University. The streamlined design was executed in buff brick with cast stone, black Carrara glass, stainless steel, and glass block. The theater entrance has curved walls, which are reflected in the semicircular marquee. The marquee incorporates metal panels, stainless steel moldings, and neon strip lighting. The "Landis" sign is made of bent metal, which is an intrinsic part of the marquee design. The original circular metal and glass ticket booth remains beneath the marquee.
The adjacent Mori Building is a commercial building constructed of the same brick detailing as the theater and was conceived as part of the complex. One of the most playful and theatrical buildings in New Jersey, the Landis Theatre is currently being renovated as a 750-seat performing arts venue.

Carnegie Library, Vineland

Vineland's Carnegie Library reflects Andrew Carnegie's aspirations for libraries to become cultural anchors for their communities. It is a massive structure constructed of random ashlar granite walls trimmed with carved limestone corner quoins, belt courses, cornices, and gable coping stones. It has a two-columned Ionic portico with full pediment marking the entrance, which is centrally located on the long side of its rectangular mass. The library is only five bays wide but has a monumental scale imparted by its raised basement, stone walls, and slate roof. It has a louvered, metal cupola that is centered on the roof and articulated by corner pilasters supporting arches. A metal dome caps the cupola. The building is still serving the community through its use as a senior center.

The Landis School, built in 1927 as the Vineland High School, has been in
continuous operation since then, though it now serves as a middle school.
James O. Betelle, a prolific architect of schools throughout New Jersey,
designed the building. Betelle formed his partnership with Ernest F. Guilbert
in Newark in 1910, after having apprenticed at the Philadelphia architectural
firm of Walter Cope and John Stewardson, recognized as popularizers, with
Ralph Adams Cram and Bertram Goodhue, of the Collegiate Gothic style.
Betelle developed a specific interest in school architecture and construction,
and was nationally renowned for his development of schools as
multipurpose buildings. At the Landis School, both the auditorium and the
gymnasium can be used independently of the classroom functions, a
farsighted innovation at the time. The school's architecture is English Gothic
Revival in style, a brick structure with limestone trim. The long entrance
façade is dominated by an asymmetrical tower, a four-story rectangular block
with an engaged octagonal turret housing a bell tower. At the main entrance
a stone pointed arch is flanked by a secondary entrance that punctures a
solitary buttress. The school is a strong architectural presence in the
community, as well as a strong cultural one, as three generations of
Vinelanders have called it their school.

Broad Street Presbyterian Church, Bridgeton

This splendid Georgian church is considered one of the finest examples of its type in the United States. At the end of the eighteenth century "Bridge Town" was a village of about fifty dwellings, located near the Delaware Bay and proximate to river trade routes. The inhabitants elected to build a church prior to the Revolution, but the war forestalled their efforts. Senator Jonathan Elmer, Colonel David Potter, General James Giles, and Mark Miller donated the land upon which to build the "meeting house." Using subscriptions from local residents, the trustees began construction on July 26, 1792. The first services were held on Sunday, December 13, 1795. The first pastor was Dr. William Clarkson, a physician who had practiced in New York City. The interior is notable for its U-shaped balcony and exquisite carved woodwork. The building was recorded by the Historic American Buildings Survey and is listed on the State and National Registers of Historic Places.

The Cumberland County Courthouse, designed by Watson and Huckel of
Philadelphia in 1909, is a monumental Classical Revival structure located in
the center of Bridgeton. Constructed of Indiana limestone, it has a Grecian
entrance portico, "distyle in muris" in the Ionic order. The structure is a
rectangular mass, two-and-one-half stories tall, with a raised granite base.
The projecting entrance portico is centered on the long wall with three
arcuated bays on either side. It has windows in small arched openings on the
ground floor and originally had six monumental arched windows in the two
courtrooms above. The large openings were blocked with limestone panels
when the two courtrooms were divided into four in 1967. A major feature of
the design is the Baroque tower that rises above the roof behind the entrance.
It features paired Ionic columns set diagonally at the corners with arched
windows in between. Above that is another floor level containing the clock,
which is capped by a bell cast copper roof surmounted by a gold weather vane.

Lighthouses

New Jersey is blessed with a large collection of historic lighthouses from Cape May to Sandy Hook. These structures range in date, size, design, and materials, but all are architectural landmarks in the truest sense of that word, as they provide orientation points for both land and sea travelers. New Jersey's oldest extant lighthouse is Sandy Hook (above), which was built in the mid-eighteenth century as an octagonal structure of whitewashed rubble stone. The largest lighthouses, at Cape May (p. 131), Barnegat (p. 132), and Absecon (p. 133), were all built in the late 1850s and constructed of brick; they range from 100 to 175 feet tall. One of the most distinctive of New Jersey's lighthouses is Twin Lights, built in 1862 on the cliffs of the Atlantic Highlands, 200 feet above sea level. Several range lights were constructed on the Delaware Bay in the late nineteenth century, including the Finn's Point Range and the Tinnicum Island Rear Range. These and other lighthouses are located in shore areas of great aesthetic beauty and are majestic built objects in their natural settings.

Whig Hall
PJ...

4

The Delaware River
Region

The Delaware River Region is defined by contrasts: the dense and gritty
cities of Trenton and Camden, with their long histories of manufacturing;
the most sparsely populated area of the state, the Pinelands; and the cultural and intellectual magnet of Princeton. Two features, the Pinelands and
the Delaware River, dominate the geography. Composed of portions of the

Inner and Outer Coastal Plains, the landscape is generally flat, with rolling hills in the northern portion of the region, where the topography changes to the Piedmont.

Quakers came early to this area. Their settlements and influence are profoundly felt throughout the region. In addition to their wonderful architectural legacy, the Quaker population here, as elsewhere throughout the state, was active in the Underground Railroad, hastening the demise of slavery in the country. The Quaker meetinghouse in Woodbury (1715) is one of the oldest churches in the state and, like most meetinghouses, is built of brick.

Among the numerous small towns that offer an attractive alternative to city living are places like Haddonfield, which has one of the oldest historic districts in the state. Not far south from Camden, it offers small-town amenities close to the hustle and bustle of the city.

Camden has been the focus of significant efforts at rehabilitation, largely along its waterfront. In the Camden shipyards during World War II, battleships, aircraft carriers, destroyers, and heavy cruisers were built. Industry was prominent. These days the effort is to return life to the city in ways that provide variety and interest, making the city again a destination for young people and families.

The Pine Barrens, named for the pine trees that grow so prolifically there and for the resulting scarcity of farms, has less attractive and productive soils than elsewhere in New Jersey. The soils are sandy, acidic, and nutrient-poor. What little agriculture exists there has centered on cranberry and blueberry production. One million acres of the Pine Barrens were made a National Reserve in 1978 in order to protect water quality for the region. This action restricted development and maintained the population at its sparse levels.

Trenton was established by Quakers in 1679. It was the site of Washington's first victory in the Revolutionary War and became the state capital in 1790. Like Newark and Paterson, Trenton suffered from middle-class exodus after the riots of 1968, coupled with the loss of industrial production. The state government is concentrated in the city, but most workers leave for homes in the suburbs at the end of the day. Recent years have seen efforts to reverse the long downward spiral. An instance of that effort was the long-term restoration of the state capitol building, which was a resounding success and an indication of the city's potential.

The Princeton area is a center of higher education and research, spurring development along the Route 1 corridor nearby.

Camden Waterfront

Camden's greatest physical attribute, and the focus of strenuous efforts to reverse the city's long decline, is its waterfront. Extending along the Delaware River opposite Philadelphia, Camden was once known as "the biggest little city in the world," the home of RCA Victor, Campbell Soup Company, and Walt Whitman. The contraction of manufacturing and the surge of the automobile in American life contributed to Camden's urban dilemmas. Since 1984 there has been a concerted effort, led by the Cooper's Ferry Development Association, to reshape the waterfront, in the hope that its resurgence will stimulate the revitalization of the city. The New Jersey State Aquarium, designed by Hillier Architecture, opened in 1992; after a 2005 renovation, it was renamed the Adventure Aquarium. Campbell's Field, built in 2001 as the home of the minor league Camden Riversharks baseball team, features views of the Benjamin Franklin Bridge. The Susquehanna Bank Center (formerly the Tweeter Center) is a 25,000-seat, open-air amphitheater opened in 1995. And One Port Center, by architect Michael Graves, has housed the headquarters of the Delaware River Port Authority since 1994. Ferry service to Philadelphia was resumed in 1992, and office and residential construction have further strengthened the waterfront.

One of the most elaborate of the Carnegie libraries built in New Jersey still stands in Camden, though it is now sadly in ruinous condition, with its roof collapsed into the structure, leaving only its exterior walls intact. Designed in 1905 by Hale and Morse, a prominent Philadelphia firm, the building has brick bearing walls faced with yellowish-tan Roman brick and elaborately carved limestone ornament. The façade is organized much like a triumphal arch from antiquity. The building has a four-columned portico of the Ionic order with Scamozzi capitals. The arched entryway has a bracketed keystone, which is contained by a projecting pediment articulated by modillions. The carved limestone tympanum sculpture depicts garlands, cornucopia, and fruit. The original iron lanterns are mounted on the stone cheek walls of the monumental stair. The brick walls have recessed panels bordered at the edge by limestone quoins. The building originally had a hipped roof hidden behind a raised stone parapet wall. It is most unfortunate that this building was allowed by the city and the state to deteriorate to the point of collapse. Fortunately, a recent grant for exterior restoration may facilitate this library's preservation for another use.

The RCA Victor Building in Camden, also known as the "Nipper Building," is one of New Jersey's most important and recognizable industrial landmarks. Designed in 1909 by Ballinger and Perrot, this enormous structure has served as a visual landmark for the city since its construction on the waterfront. It was a manufacturing plant for phonograph players and other electrical equipment. The main mass of the building is a six-story industrial loft structure, which is vaguely classical in design. It has a rusticated brick base and brick piers running the full height of the building. Expansive metal windows open between the piers, headed by cast stone lintels and brick spandrel panels that extend to the sills of the windows of the next floor. The walls are capped by a decorative, corbelled brick cornice. An exuberantly detailed tower extends five stories above the sixth floor and is articulated by brick buttresses at the corners with limestone trim. In addition to projecting balconies at an intermediate level, the tower has what appears to be a top level for a clockworks. But instead of clock faces on all four sides, the round openings contain huge stained glass panels depicting the dog Nipper looking into the horn of a phonograph player, which is the visual symbol for "his master's voice," the company's slogan. The building was recently renovated as condominium loft apartments, which saved it from demolition. It is now a vital component of the new Camden waterfront.

After participating actively in the founding of the United States, the
Freemasons continued to prosper well into the twentieth century, offering
camaraderie to legions of men in "lodges" or "temples" in urban areas.
Membership peaked during the first decades of the twentieth century,
spurring the construction of many elaborate buildings throughout the United
States. The largest, such as the Temple of the Scottish Rite in Collingswood,
often featured theaters, classrooms, banquet halls, and other public
facilities. If some large temples have languished in recent years, the
Collingswood building has become a preservation success story. It was
purchased by the city and converted into a performing arts center ten years
ago and now offers a full range of concerts throughout the week.

Trenton's Fire Department was founded in 1747, making it one of the oldest in the United States. Today the department protects the state capital, a city of 88,000 residents and 25,000 daily workers, mainly state employees. In 2002 the department moved into a new headquarters building designed by Venturi, Scott Brown and Associates, the famed Philadelphia firm. Robert Venturi had designed a fire station for the city in the 1960s that was never built, so this commission may well have seemed like a homecoming. The 54,000-square-foot building incorporates a fire museum in an older wing, designed by Hunt and Kelly, as well as facilities for Ladder Company 10 and workshops for equipment maintenance. The "supergraphic" sign with a fireman's hat that floats like a ribbon on the façade of the building is a nod to the famous BASCO store from the 1970s and other Venturi "decorated sheds."

In 1848 John Roebling purchased a twenty-five-acre site along the Delaware and Raritan Canal in Chambersburg for his wire rope business. Roebling designed the buildings and machinery and directed the company until his death in 1869, when his three sons, Washington, Ferdinand, and Charles, took over. Charles Roebling subsequently designed the buildings and machinery until his death in 1918. Roebling cable was used in suspension bridges throughout the world, including the Brooklyn Bridge and the Bear Mountain Bridge. By World War I, the Roebling complex was the largest wire rope plant in the world. The different building types in the plant show the evolution of rebuilding campaigns linked to major bridge projects and to war production. The earliest extant building is Wire Mill #4, dating from 1871, which has been saved and sits opposite a new indoor arena that replaced other buildings in the complex. The County of Mercer occupies the former administrative office buildings on South Broad Street (circa 1920), and the Housing and Mortgage Finance Agency of the State of New Jersey has converted the former wire rope shop behind them to serve as its headquarters. Other planned adaptive uses of the industrial buildings include a museum, shopping centers, schools, and loft housing.

The Capitol Complex in Trenton is the second oldest state capitol in continuous use (after Maryland's). A segment of the original State House building designed in 1792 by Jonathan Doane still exists in the Governor's Wing, although it was extensively renovated in the late nineteenth century. The building went through major alterations in the mid-nineteenth century by the architects John Notman and Samuel Sloan. However, most of the building as it currently exists dates from the twenty years around the turn of the twentieth century. The Assembly Chamber was designed by James Moylan in 1893, and the Senate Chamber was added by Arnold Moses in 1905. The front section, the dome, and the rotunda, which constitute the present image of the building, were designed in 1895 by Lewis Broom, who also designed the city hall in Jersey City. The Capitol Complex includes the State House Annex, which was designed for the judicial branch in the 1920s by Hunt and Kelly. It is a Neoclassical limestone building of high quality and contains elaborate courtrooms and other public spaces now used as hearing rooms for the legislature. In the 1960s the complex was expanded significantly to the west by the Grad Partnership of Newark to include the cultural complex, which consists of the State Library, State Museum, an auditorium, and a planetarium. The most recent additions to the complex were made in the mid-1990s during a major restoration project designed by the joint venture of Short & Ford and Johnson Jones. They include a granite-faced legislative staff building, a below-grade parking garage, and the development of new visitor accommodations beneath a public plaza between the State House and Annex.

Grounds for Sculpture, Hamilton

One of the most intriguing and provocative sites in New Jersey is the
Grounds for Sculpture. As conceived by the philanthropist and sculptor
J. Seward Johnson, the intention was to create a place where the public
could experience large-scale sculpture informally in a pleasing setting.
Designed by landscape architect Allan Goodheart and architect Kevin Wilkes,
the site opened in 1992 on the former New Jersey State Fairgrounds.
The permanent collection boasts more than 240 works, including pieces by
established artists like George Segal, by emerging artists, and by Johnson
himself. Not insignificantly, the landscape of the park is a principal element
of the experience, punctuated by the reused state fair buildings. The design
and maintenance of the landscape contribute greatly to the presentation of
the sculpture. The site is unquestionably the finest public sculpture garden
in the state.

This building is the first commissioned work in the United States by well-known British architect Richard Rogers (b. 1933). Built in 1982, it was one of the first buildings to use its structural steel frame as an expressive feature of the design. This concept of an exoskeleton was explored earlier in Rogers's work with Renzo Piano (b. 1937) at the Centre Pompidou in Paris. In the PA Technology Center, the exposed triangular structural towers and cables support column-free work areas to either side. The centrally located towers are arrayed like high-tension power lines and support a continuous platform above the roof of the occupied space that holds mechanical, electrical, and plumbing equipment. Beneath the platform is the main circulation spine of the building, with laboratories and offices to each side. The exterior envelope of the work areas consists of translucent Kalwall panels that contain smaller, transparent windows. The original bright red color of the structure has now faded to pink and needs to be repainted to regain the full effect of the design. Other than the faded colors, the design still appears contemporary and innovative; and the building maintains a strong architectural presence in its open suburban setting.

The Bath House is widely regarded as a turning point in architect Louis Kahn's career, the first realization of his concept of "servant" and "served" spaces, which he further developed in such projects as the Richards Medical Center, the Salk Institute, and the Kimbell Art Museum. Icons of modern American architecture, Kahn's Trenton Bath House (1955) and Day Camp Pavilions (1957) were commissioned by the Trenton Jewish Community Center and designed as crisp geometric forms within a proportional, ordered landscape. Kahn also designed a community center building, a central green framed by trees, and tree-lined parking lots, but these elements were not constructed. The Bath House has a Greek cross plan with pyramidal roofs floating over the cinder-block demising walls. The roofs are in turn anchored to the concrete slabs of the "servant" elements, which form baffled entries into the dressing rooms or separate toilet rooms within the dressing areas. The entrance to the Bath House was marked by a mural painted by Kahn's staff depicting aquatic motifs. The original design for the central atrium called for a circular spray pool, which was never fully constructed. The four Day Camp Pavilions were designed to resemble a group of Greek temples and were built with concrete-filled sewer pipes for columns and precast concrete planks forming the roofs. The entire site has now been conveyed to Ewing Township for use as a community and senior center, and the Kahn work will be restored and maintained for its original uses.

Nassau Hall stands at the literal and figurative heart of Princeton University and currently houses the offices of the president and upper administration. Originally, it was the only building for the College of New Jersey and housed students, faculty, classrooms, a chapel, and a dining hall. Designed by Robert Smith and completed by 1757, it was twice destroyed by fire and rebuilt to the designs of Benjamin Latrobe in 1810 and John Notman in 1855. It briefly served as the colonial capitol when the Continental Congress met in Princeton during the Revolutionary War in 1783. One of the nation's most important early academic buildings, it was constructed of indigenous brownstone in the Georgian style, with three front doorways with flat arches and stone quoins. After the second major fire, the building was rebuilt according to the "fireproof" construction of the day: iron support beams, arched brick floor structure, and brick walls finished with plaster. The front façade was given a projecting central pediment with a monumental stone entryway, new Italianate lanterns that capped new stone stairways at each end of the building, and a high, open cupola at the center of the roof containing a bell and topped by a copper dome surmounted by a lantern. Although the lanterns were seen as "old-fashioned" at the turn of the twentieth century and removed, Notman's version of Nassau Hall is essentially that which survives today.

Whig Hall is a Greek Revival temple of the Doric order designed by
A. Page Brown in 1895. It was built as one of two matching buildings behind
Nassau Hall that housed the rival campus debating groups, the Whig and
Cliosophical Societies. These buildings of Vermont marble replaced smaller
and earlier wood frame temples on the same sites. In 1970 the interior of
Whig Hall was destroyed by fire. It was rebuilt in the modernist idiom by
Charles Gwathmey (1938–2009), one of the "New York Five," five architects
who explored formal issues in similar ways and whose 1967 Museum of
Modern Art exhibition and subsequent book caused a stir (the others were
Richard Meier, Michael Graves, John Hejduk, and Peter Eisenman). At Whig,
the original east wall was removed, and the marble end columns were made
to serve as a frame for a concrete and glass insertion into the classical
context. The solution won many design awards and merited international
publication and interest. Another renovation in 2009 by Farewell Mills
Gatsch Architects made many functional and systems improvements to the
building while restoring the essence of the Gwathmey design and preserving
original 1895 fabric.

Blair Hall was designed by Walter Cope and John Stewardson in 1897. It is one of the largest and finest of the Collegiate Gothic undergraduate dormitories at Princeton University and one of the earliest examples of this style in the country. The Collegiate Gothic style quickly came to be associated with academe. Campuses across the country began cloaking their buildings with features that evoked an intellectual and cultural connection to the bastions of English education, Oxford and Cambridge. Given by railroad magnate John Insley Blair, Blair Hall was modeled after Bryn Mawr College's Rockefeller Hall, designed by the same architects. Blair Hall has a distinctive large tower, which is set at an angle between dormitory wings and articulated by four crenellated turrets at the corners. When it was built, the tower served as the main entrance to the campus from the railroad station that existed below it. A great stair rises up from the lower courtyard to a grand archway in the tower. The interior of the building contains oak stairways, fireplace mantels and paneling, and doors. It was renovated in recent years to gain additional living space under the high roofs. Although the railroad station has been moved farther south, the building still serves as a gateway to campus. The view from the lower courtyard toward the stair and tower is one of the iconic images of Princeton University.

In their second project for Princeton University, begun in 1899, Walter Cope and John Stewardson extended their Gothic vision to the south of Blair Hall by building Stafford Little Hall, a long and narrow Collegiate Gothic structure that zigzags south to Dillon Gymnasium. Its interior woodwork and architectural details are very similar to those of Blair Hall. A large square tower with a crenellated corner turret stands toward the north end of the building. The exterior is articulated by Tudor brick chimneystacks, slate roofs, and limestone corner blocks and window trim. It presents a picturesque appearance and a graceful human scale, which is a counterpoint to its monumental neighbor to the north. The fact that the entrances to the dormitory rooms are all on the eastern side is an indication that the building originally turned its back to the former railroad tracks to the west. Little Hall now defines and borders beautiful courtyards on both the east and the west.

One of the most beautiful Gothic chapels in the United States, the Princeton University Chapel is a masterpiece of ecclesiastical design and perhaps the best church in the extensive liturgical oeuvre of Ralph Adams Cram. As the university's supervising architect from 1907 to 1929, Cram had a significant hand in defining the appearance of the campus. At the time of its dedication in 1928, this university chapel was second in size only to King's College Chapel at Cambridge. The massive profile of the chapel is visible for miles to the south and east of campus. Its dimensions are 270 feet long by 61 feet wide and 120 feet tall. The building was constructed of a variegated Pennsylvania stone called Roaring Run sandstone, which is trimmed with carved Indiana limestone. The carved ornament is highly decorative and includes pinnacles, finials, quatrefoil motifs, and sculptural relief. The stained glass windows are among the most significant of the period and include works by Henry Willet, Charles Connick, H. W. Goodhue, and Wilbur Herbert Burnham. Subjects include: the Second Coming of Christ, Christ the teacher, Christian discipline, the Love of Christ, and epic windows such as the Divine Comedy, Morte d'Arthur, and Paradise Lost. The interior carved oak woodwork, organ casing, and pews complete an ensemble that is an artistic achievement of the highest order.

The Princeton University Graduate College is the masterpiece of Collegiate Gothic architecture designed by Ralph Adams Cram (1863–1942), the most important proponent of modern Gothic in the United States. He lectured widely on the subject and wrote many books, such as *The Substance of Gothic* (1917), in which he proselytized the beauty and appropriateness of the style. The location and design of the college was the culmination of a struggle between University President Woodrow Wilson, who wanted the college to be a part of the central campus, and the first dean of the Graduate College, Andrew Fleming West, who prevailed with the trustees on the present location at the golf course, about a mile away. The dispute led Wilson to resign and to begin his political career as the governor of New Jersey and ultimately as president of the United States. The initial stages of the complex, completed in 1913, consisted of more than 150,000 square feet of space for dormitory suites, common social areas, the impressive Gothic dining room (Procter Hall), and Cleveland Memorial Tower, the tallest Gothic tower in Princeton at 173 feet. The North Court, which includes Van Dyke Library and additional dormitory rooms, was added in 1928. Both dormitory areas were constructed of a sedimentary stone called Lockatong argillite that was quarried locally. Most of the decorative trim was constructed of carved Indiana limestone. In addition, Cleveland Tower is trimmed with quoins made of Wissahickon schist from a quarry in suburban Philadelphia. Procter Hall is graced with a hammerbeam ceiling similar to that of Westminster Abbey and stained glass from two of the finest studios in the United States: Charles Connick of Boston and the Willet Studio of Philadelphia. The latter firm executed the monumental Seven Liberal Arts window in the gable end behind the high table.

Robertson Hall is the signature building of the Woodrow Wilson School at Princeton University. Designed by Minoru Yamasaki (1912–1986) and built in 1966, the 90,000-square-foot structure houses the core functions of the School of Public and International Affairs, including classrooms, auditoria, a gallery, a cafeteria, and offices for faculty and administration. Its most distinctive feature is the monumental colonnade that wraps all four sides of the building. Derisively called the "bike rack," the colonnade is similar to the vaguely Gothic screen of columns that decorated another of Yamasaki's major works, the World Trade Center. The building is situated as a classically planned temple on a high, landscaped plateau. Entrances are centrally located on the long sides of the building. The façades are articulated in white travertine with base, columns, and an attic story that functions as an entablature. To the north is a sunken granite plaza containing a reflecting pool, which is a campus landmark. The singularity of the design meant that additions to render the building more functional had to be made underground and are hidden beneath the lawn. Now at almost fifty years of age, Robertson Hall is considered to be a mid-twentieth-century icon, an attempt at "monumental" architecture in a modernist idiom.

Koetter-Kim and Associates designed the 50,000-square-foot addition to Firestone Library in 1988 for additional stack space, offices, and reading rooms. The addition expanded the lowest levels of the library originally built in 1948. The slope of the site falls away from the campus toward Nassau Street, where the upper stone walls of the addition, which match those of the main building, emerge from the ground. This plinth-like form creates a low garden wall and open space parallel to Nassau Street that is landscaped to form a linear public plaza along the sidewalk. At the northeast corner of the composition, a low, semi-circular tower with a sloping glass roof brings light into the spaces below. The interior is articulated with metal trusses, exposed stone walls, and glass skylights. The skylights illuminate the reading rooms with natural light that enhances the expansiveness of the spaces beneath. While the building is complete in itself, its form seems to anticipate future additional floors that could be built above it.

Gordon Wu Hall was the first and most significant of Robert Venturi's numerous buildings on the Princeton campus. Planned in 1980 as part of the university's conversion to a residential college system, Wu Hall was created to serve as the dining hall and social center of Butler College, a converted group of 1950s dormitory buildings. Its site, at the junction of two major campus walks, challenged the architect to knit disparate spaces and masses together, and the result was one of his most widely admired works. Finished in 1983, the building stands today as a modest link between "old Princeton" and the spectacular new campus erected with vast alumni wealth during the past twenty-five years. It has worn well during the more than quarter century since its completion, proving that the architect's concept of a threshold from Collegiate Gothic to Modernism was an appropriate response to both time and place. A number of subsequent academic buildings have followed its precedent.

The four-story, 110,000-square-foot Lewis Thomas Laboratory on the
Princeton University campus was named in honor of the molecular biologist
and author, who was a member of the Princeton class of 1933. The molecular
biology laboratories were designed in 1986 by Payette Associates, a firm that
specialized in laboratory design. The elaborately detailed brick and cast
stone envelope was designed by Robert Venturi (b. 1925), Princeton class
of 1947, and one of the country's most influential living architects. Venturi
popularized the notion of the "decorated shed," of which this building is an
excellent example. He adds visual interest and human scale to what could
have been a monotonous laboratory building by manipulating colors and
patterns in the brickwork and cast stone. The long elevations are articulated
by metal windows with transoms that create a consistent rhythm for the
bottom three stories. The top floor is decorated with square patterns that
break down the scale of this tall space, which houses mechanical and
laboratory ventilation equipment. This lively composition won a national
AIA Honor Award in 1987.

157

Feinberg Hall is part of the Wilson Hall residential college at Princeton University. It was designed by Princeton alumnus Tod Williams (b. 1943) and Billie Tsien (b. 1949), who have completed many campus buildings of distinction, including the Natatorium at the Cranbrook Academy in Bloomfield Hills, Michigan. Feinberg Hall is an interpretation of a Gothic tower that creates a new focal point amid the many low-scale and horizontal dormitory buildings at the south end of campus. This 40-by- 40-foot building is 80 feet high and five stories tall. Constructed of brick and

concrete block, with concrete plank floors, it has rich texture imparted by the colors and scale of its materials. Its most distinctive features are the steeply pitched, copper clad roof and the inverted steel and wire glass canopy over the main stair. The four-person suites have commanding views and have led Feinberg Hall to be nicknamed "the fishbowl." The massing and detailing of the building are interesting and active, and the plan fulfills the functional requirements of a modern dormitory in a creative way. The building received an AIA Honor Award for design excellence in 1988.

The Princeton Public Library was founded in 1909 and for many years was accommodated in Bainbridge House, now the home of the Historical Society of Princeton. The current building on the corner of Witherspoon and Wiggins Streets was designed by Hillier Architecture and built in 2004. It replaced an earlier and much-loved modernist structure designed in 1966. Although there was concern about losing the prior building, the new library has now been embraced as a community landmark. This three-story brick, glass, and metal structure is articulated by monumental, round brick columns that rise the full height of the building, with glass curtain walls between them. A four-story entrance pavilion at the southwest corner has projecting metal and glass canopies and is capped by a glass lantern with a glass wing roof that floats above it. The materials and transparency of the façades make the building warm and inviting to its users. It contains public art by local artists like Robert Barry, Katherine Hackl, and Margaret Johnson. The library's construction sparked the creation of a new civic space in the heart of Princeton consisting of a landscaped plaza with outdoor tables that serve the surrounding restaurants and coffee shops.

The former Witherspoon School for Colored Children is in the John
Witherspoon neighborhood of Princeton, an area originally settled by freed
slaves. Still populated primarily by African Americans, the neighborhood was
home to Paul Robeson, who attended the Witherspoon School. In compliance
with state law, the school was desegregated in 1947 and remained in use for
grades six through eight until 1968. In 2002 Robert Hillier purchased the
building and began plans to transform it into a mixed-income residential
property with thirty-four apartments. Respectful of the former school's
cultural importance to the community, Hillier Architecture maintained the
general interior layout while providing a mix of one- and two-bedroom units:
ceilings were returned to their original twelve-foot height, windows that had
been partially obscured were restored, and the brick façade was repointed.
The project was named The Waxwood in honor of Howard B. Waxwood Jr.,
the principal who presided over the school's integration. A small park was
created on-site to provide outdoor public space, a boon in such a dense
community. A foundation established by the developer provides financial
assistance to long-time residents of the community, lessening the impact of
gentrification. The renovation, completed in 2005, is listed on the National
Register of Historic Places.

A recent phenomenon in urban redevelopment has been the resurgence of "old-tyme" downtown baseball parks. Three have been built in recent years in New Jersey's major cities: Trenton (above), Newark (p. 162, top), and Camden (p. 162, bottom). All three of these parks are impressively situated along rivers at former industrial sites in their downtown areas.

They are mid-size, minor league stadiums that accommodate 5,000 to 10,000 fans, allowing them to get close to the action and root for players who may ascend to the major leagues.

These parks are framed with exposed structural steel and have brick walls, precast concrete grandstands, and decorative metal trim. They have generous areas for entertainment, concessions, and support services, and contain picnic areas for parties and special occasions. Large electronic scoreboards with sound and video complement the aesthetic experience. These are places where parents can take their children at an affordable price and experience America's pastime with a hot dog and a soft drink.

High Point
BKG

5
The Skylands Region

The Skylands Region is commonly known as the Highlands because its topography is the most rugged and varied in the state. Its physiographic regions are the Ridge and Valley (adjacent to the Delaware River), the Highlands (foothills of the Appalachian chain), and the Piedmont (which contains some of the oldest rocks on the continent).

The north and west portions of the region are less densely populated than other parts of the state, and their attractions relate directly to the sense of openness and rural character. Here one encounters small towns and places for outdoor recreation. The Delaware Water Gap and the riverside towns extending downstream toward, and including, Lambertville are among these jewels.

Farther east, the county seats of Somerville, Morristown, and Flemington exert their influence. Encircling these municipal centers are smaller towns and villages, now almost universally connected by the roadside developments that collectively define the suburbanization of America for good and ill. For at least fifty years development has held sway here, turning pastures into subdivisions and cutting swaths of interstate highways through the countryside. Among the newest battles to be waged in the state is how future development will be permitted to occur, as ecological concerns run up against the engine of capitalism. The Skylands Region may prove to be an indicator of the American future, as the arguments aired here, and the choices made, will be cited throughout the country.

The energy expended in expansion over the recent past has been outwardly directed, that is, toward development of new land. Even though the negative aspect of this development has been an excessive reduction in farmland and open space, one benefit may have been the unwitting conservation of existing buildings, especially within urban centers. Consequently, in some instances precious architectural resources have been allowed to survive.

This region is renowned for having sustained George Washington's New Jersey campaign during the Revolutionary War. Morristown National Historical Park includes the scattered sites of Washington's Headquarters at the Ford Mansion, Fort Nonsense, and Jockey Hollow park. Today, the region has become a technology center, known for AT&T and Verizon and for pharmaceutical companies, including Johnson & Johnson, Wyeth, Pfizer, Sanofi-Aventis, Novartis, and Merck.

Despite New Jersey's reputation as a paved and highly trafficked state, it is worth noting that the Skylands Region is home to the U.S. Professional Golf Association (housed in a former residence by John Russell Pope in Far Hills) and the U.S. Equestrian Team Foundation (at Hamilton Farm in Gladstone). In an age of constant and rapidly expanding technology, it is comforting to know that it is still possible to attend polo matches and take hot-air balloon rides over preserved open land.

Completed in 1829, the building is one of the oldest surviving county courthouses in New Jersey. The plan and overall design was likely taken from one of several pattern books of the period by Asher Benjamin. It has a projecting Doric portico made of bricks stuccoed to simulate stone blocks. The façades are also of stucco lined out to resemble coursed ashlar. The one large courtroom is located on the upper floor, reached by a double-run, monumental stair that rises from the front entrance hall. Other courts-related offices were accommodated in rooms arranged on either side of a double-loaded corridor on the ground floor. While its age alone imbues this courthouse with historic significance, an event took place in 1935 that focused the world's attention on the building. In January and February of that year, the Lindbergh baby kidnapping trial was held in Flemington, and the accused murderer, Bruno Hauptmann, was held in the adjacent 1925 jail. The courthouse interior was "colonialized" in several building campaigns after the trial, but it has been recently restored to its late Victorian period to reflect the significance of that event to the building's history.

Bachman-Wilson House, Millstone

The Bachman-Wilson House, a Frank Lloyd Wright design built in 1954, has no basement, attic, or garage and is, therefore, typical of Wright's Usonian houses. It differs, however, in that its bedrooms are on a second floor. This strategy reduces the length of the house and allows the living space to be two stories high. Despite its compact size, its generous ceiling height and its expansive wall of glass facing the Millstone River generate a sense of spaciousness. A patio runs the length of the glass wall, serving as a physical link between inside and out. Plywood screens at the clerestory provide inexpensive ornament and cast pleasing shadows. The house has undergone a long-term restoration by Tarantino Studios, its architect-owners, is listed on the National Register of Historic Places, and is a contributing structure to the Millstone Historic District.

This courthouse was designed by James Reily Gordon with Everts Tracy and Edgarton Swartout, all alumni of the office of McKim, Mead and White, one of the principal proponents of Beaux Arts classicism. Like the Essex County Courthouse in Newark, it is an excellent example of the American Renaissance period. A public building of modest size (about 35,000 square feet), it has a grand scale imparted by a high basement and a cascade of marble steps from the main floor down to grade. Its monumental Ionic portico and lantern capped by a copper dome with the *Statue of Enlightenment* reinforce this scale. The building dominates the historic Somerville Green, which also contains the Lord Memorial Fountain by John Russell Pope and a historic stone church used now as a jury waiting area. The interior has a full height rotunda with a circular colonnade of the Corinthian order at the level of the main courtroom. The courtroom is articulated with a judge's bench, witness area, jury area, paneling, and seats, all constructed of oak. The vaulted plaster ceiling features a large stained glass laylight in the center of the room. The room beneath the main court was fitted out as a courtroom in the 1950s, and its finishes were recently restored to that period. The entire building underwent a major renovation by Short & Ford & Partners, Architects, in the mid-1990s that refurbished the marble façade, the metal roofs, the dome, and all interior features.

In the early 1970s, at the height—or perhaps it was the end—of a celebrated history as a telecommunications giant, the largest monopoly in the world, AT&T, built its world headquarters in Basking Ridge. Local citizens had just recently prevented the Great Swamp from being paved over for an international airport, and Interstate 287 did not yet run as far north as Morristown. Here, next to a swamp and in the middle of small communities, AT&T erected an ensemble of seven connected buildings, totaling 2.7 million square feet on 140 acres, designed by Vincent Kling of Philadelphia. Little expense was spared. The parking garage could accommodate 3,900 cars. A waterfall cascaded in the interior. Pitched roofs were protected with clay tiles. The company's totem, the statue *Spirit of Communication,* nicknamed "Golden Boy," was brought from Manhattan and ensconced in its new home. Such massive construction could have decimated the natural surroundings, but the complex is handsome, and its insertion into the countryside was handled very skillfully. Its sheltering and interrupted roofline mitigates the collective bulk, and its rolling landscape helps screen its lower floors from view. Also important to New Jersey was the effect the arrival of AT&T had on the development of the suburban countryside. AT&T's presence in the seeming hinterlands legitimized the practice, and soon every interstate interchange was populated by office buildings.

Located in the exclusive Somerset Hills on the upper Raritan River, Blairsden was built from 1898 to 1900—the heyday of country life in America. The American plutocracy of the *fin-de-siècle* owned a staggering chunk of the nation's wealth and used its capital to build lavish estates on the best sites in the New York area. C. Ledyard Blair, the builder of Blairsden, was a railroad and financial tycoon who controlled the Erie-Lackawanna Railroad, among other lines. After purchasing 625 acres in Peapack, he had a spur built to the village in order to make his daily commute from home to the Blair and Company Building in Manhattan. The architects of the house were John Carrère and Thomas Hastings, partners in one of the premier Beaux Arts firms in the country and the designers of the New York Public Library. In this, their finest extant country house, they employed the same rich palette of materials and modern technology that went into their design for Henry Clay Frick's home in New York City (now the Frick Museum). After its sale by the Blair family in 1950, the estate was used as a religious retreat for Catholic women for half a century. A private conservancy dedicated to the preservation of outstanding classical houses purchased the house recently and is working to restore it.

The corporate offices designed for Beneficial Corporation's headquarters in Peapack were a departure when the site was developed in the mid-1980s. The architecture seeks to evoke academic villages like the Universities of Virginia, Richmond, and Delaware, with its campus organized around landscaped, outdoor rooms and Colonial details. The result is a strong effort to establish a workplace that not only has a stable, recognizable identity, but also celebrates the idea of community. Designed by the Hillier Group, the assemblage of buildings is accurately described as a campus, a deliberate attempt to create not only a collection of buildings, but also a coherent series of outdoor spaces. Instead of concentrating workspaces in one or two buildings with extremely large floor areas, the office buildings are relatively modest in size, and their rectangular proportions permit daylight to penetrate deeply into the interior spaces. These structures are connected by a combination of interior and exterior elements, as illustrated by the arcade and clock tower pictured above. The notion of campus is further developed by the use of a stripped-down, traditional architectural style, vaguely Colonial Revival, rendered in brick. Within the last decade, Pfizer took over the former Beneficial Corporation property, and in October 2009 Pfizer acquired Wyeth. Although Pfizer will close its facility in Bridgewater, the Peapack and Madison offices will remain open.

When asked where a client should go to buy property for a house, Frank Lloyd
Wright is reported to have said, "Go as far away from the city as possible, and
when you get there, keep going." Whether or not the anecdote is true, the
sentiment squares with Wright's desire to connect his designs with the land.
The James B. Christie House was built in 1940 on an eleven-acre parcel of
woodland where two streams join before running a short way into the Passaic
River. Not far from Jockey Hollow, where Washington's troops wintered in
1779–1780, the area remains largely unchanged since the house was built.
An L-shaped Usonian house, the Christie House shares substantial features
with the 1,200-square-foot Pope-Leighey House, now located at Woodlawn
Plantation in Alexandria, Virginia. The Christie House, though barely 2,000
square feet, is the largest of the three Wright-designed Usonians in New Jersey.
The living room opens onto a long patio overlooking a sweep of lawn that
drops to the trees and the streams. It features plywood screens at clerestory
windows and a compact dining area. It is approached at the hinge of the L to
protect and control the view. The Christie House was built by Harold Turner,
who criss-crossed the country between 1937 and 1943, building various
Usonian houses. In the process, he became masterful at creating the millwork
Wright's designs required. His skill is evident in the finish work here. The
house escaped demolition after the property was subdivided in the mid-1980s,
and it retains its initial quirky character and charm in a private setting.

Wyeth Headquarters, Madison

The former Geraldine R. Dodge estate in Madison is the site of a planned office development known as Giralda Farms. Consisting of 175 acres near the campuses of Fairleigh Dickinson and Drew Universities, the development was envisioned as a series of high-quality but low-profile sites. Only seven sites were defined, and 85 percent of the land was required to be left as open space. Most automobile parking is underground, and the large setbacks from the road ensure that the development, accessed from only two gates, appears parklike. American Home Products, now known as Wyeth (and purchased by Pfizer in 2009), built its corporate headquarters here.
The office building, designed by the Hillier Group, is arranged as a series of three nearly square boxes facing east, slightly set back from one another and connected by a long, narrow building on the west. At the north end of the longer building, an elongated box contains the public entry. The entire building is three stories high. Its four boxes are clad in brick and have individual window openings, while the connecting building is sheathed in glass. This contrast of materials and forms reduces the building's apparent length while providing visual interest. The result is a sedate and sophisticated building located in an enviably bucolic setting.

One of the finest Georgian houses in New Jersey, the Ford Mansion was erected in 1774 by Colonel Jacob Ford on a prominence that afforded views over the countryside in all directions, including Morristown to the west. The house is one of the most historically significant in the nation, having served as George Washington's military headquarters from December 1779 to June 1780 during the harshest recorded winter in New Jersey history. Amazingly, only 100 soldiers died during that winter, as opposed to the 3,000 who died at Valley Forge two years earlier; improved winter preparations and inoculations for smallpox account for the difference. The main section of the house is two-and-one-half stories tall and capped by a pitched, wood shingle roof pierced by end wall chimneys. The house is five bays wide and two rooms deep, with a grand center reception hall running from front to back. It has a central Palladian entry with an arched transom over the main paneled door, with sidelights between applied pilasters. The front façade has flush board siding to simulate coursed ashlar, and it has twelve-over-twelve window sashes, typical for the period. The large, high-ceilinged formal rooms on the ground floor contain paneled walls and fireplaces, and many bedrooms fill the second floor of the main section and the kitchen wing to the east. The house is a historic museum operated by the National Park Service.

When walking the Morristown Green, it is useful to remember that the town was founded in the 1720s by wayward Presbyterians used to the Puritan ways of New England. The original common at the center of the village was the site of a tavern and a church, the two essential buildings in any New England town. The trapezoidal form of the space was the result of a spoke-like street layout in which roads ran outward in all directions to neighboring villages. The northeast side of the Green was always the site of the Presbyterian church. As the town grew in wealth and population during the nineteenth century, parishioners demanded a larger and more modern facility. Responding perhaps to the Episcopalians, who built Saint Peter's Church with Charles McKim in the late 1880s, the vestry retained the prominent New York architect Josiah William Cady (1837–1919) to create an elaborate new church in 1893. Consecrated on September 9, 1894, the massive limestone church was unusual in several ways. Cady placed the building forty feet north of the previous church, which had dominated the Green for a century, and located the nave to the east of a detached bell tower. As if to give it a more recessive presence, he also turned the nave 180 degrees, placing an apsidal volume on the Green instead of an entrance portal. As the designer of the old Metropolitan Opera House and several theaters, Cady was intent on giving worshipers a full view of the pulpit and a live acoustic for music. In this, as in several of his later church designs, he created a sweeping, semicircular auditorium instead of the standard longitudinal nave common in Calvinist worship spaces. The church complex, which includes four buildings on the Green, is still a dominant presence in Morristown, despite major changes on the south side of the park, the result of a recent redevelopment campaign.

This townhouse development, designed by Jerome Morley Larson Sr. and consisting of ninety units built between 1982 and 1987, was conceived as a group of English-style manors surrounding a walled entrance court. The massing of each cluster ranges from three stories at the center to single-story units at each end. Punctuated by engaged chimneys and tower elements, the buildings present a picturesque appearance in spite of being designed for the automobile age. Each residence opens onto a golf course at the rear.

Gustav Stickley (1858–1942) is generally considered to be the father of the Arts and Crafts movement in America. Many Garden State residents do not know that the only historic site directly connected with this seminal figure is located on a well-traveled stretch of Route 10 in Morris County. From 1910 to 1914, Stickley lived, worked, and dreamed at the place he would call Craftsman Farms, constructing a dozen buildings that are largely extant today. The Log House, in the photograph, is a prime repository of original Stickley furniture and craft artifacts. Following its preservation in 1989 and its designation as a National Historic Landmark, Craftsman Farms has emerged as a major museum and historic site, largely through state and county historic preservation grants and individual contributions. A mecca for decorative arts collectors and students of the Arts and Crafts movement, it now rivals Washington's Headquarters as one of Morris County's must-see tourist destinations.

The Morris Canal was New Jersey's contribution to the transportation revolution that drove commerce and industry in the early Republic. Constructed from 1825 to 1831, the canal had a vertical rise and fall of 1,674 feet, still the largest in the world. Of the many villages along the canal between Newark and Phillipsburg, Waterloo remains the only site with an intact lock, canal section, and buildings. Two visionary preservationists, Lou Gualandi and Percival Leach, saved the village during the 1960s, raising funds for building conservation and operating a museum/cultural center for more than twenty-five years. It was the site of classical, pop, and rock concerts, the Dodge Poetry Festival, and many other successful cultural events. Unfortunately, following Gualandi's death in 1988, the Waterloo Foundation for the Arts foundered. Poor management, financial troubles, and a series of controversial deals between private corporations and the State of New Jersey put the site at risk by 2006. When the state ceased its financial support for Waterloo Village, the foundation folded. Today the picturesque village is open on sporadic occasions as part of Allamuchy State Park, but has ceased to function as a historic museum and music venue.

High Point State Park, as the name implies, occupies the highest elevation of land in the state. The land for the park was donated by Colonel Anthony and Susie Dryden Kuser in 1923. Located on the Appalachian Trail in Sussex County, the park is carved out of forested wilderness and contains campgrounds, swimming areas on Lake Marcia, bridle paths, and hiking trails. The landscape design was by Olmsted Brothers. At the apex of the park, a 220-foot obelisk called the High Point Monument was built in 1930 in honor of all war veterans. The monument was designed by Marion Sims Wyeth (1889–1982), a graduate of Princeton University and the École des Beaux Arts, who apprenticed in the office of Carrère and Hastings. The view from the monument is 1,803 feet above sea level and overlooks a panorama of rich farmland and forests from the ridges of the Poconos to the west, the Catskills to the north, and the Wallkill Valley to the southeast.
One of the most beautiful of our state's parks, High Point offers views from its monument and trails that are a constant source of surprise and delight.

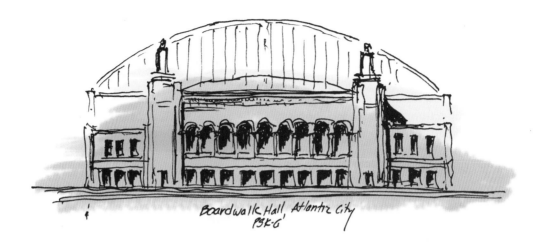

Boardwalk Hall, Atlantic City
PSK-G

Closing Thoughts

The breadth of New Jersey's architectural quality can be read in the chronology of these entries, spanning as they do from the 1700s through the 1900s to the present day. The variety of the work is evident in the divergence of scales—from small, rough suggestions of the intent to define a place, to multiple building complexes—and in the contrast of rich ornament with austere planes.

Reviewing the chronology, we see that the preponderance of the entries predate 1950. The implication may be that we value our distant past more than our recent history. Particularly when we understand that more buildings have been built since 1950, the percentage of older buildings in this collection becomes both more impressive and somewhat disheartening. One wonders, have we forgotten how to build well? What is it that we have lost?

Among the observations to be made upon completing the assembly of this catalogue is the absence of a number of worthy building types. The lack of any examples of patterned-end brick houses is unfortunate, as this is an especially important architectural legacy of the state. In addition, although New Jersey is commonly described as the crossroads of the American Revolution, it is striking to see so few sites related to the birth of our nation represented here. And while the book includes a variety of places defined by a collection of multiple buildings, little focus is given to those historic villages and enclaves that still remain.

Agrarian buildings, specifically barns, are noticeably absent from this collection. When we recognize that the role of agriculture in the state has waned nearly to the point of extinction and that disuse contributes to a building's extinction, it is not surprising that these outbuildings are not plentiful. Nevertheless, the distinctive characteristics of the German barns of western New Jersey deserve mention, as do the Dutch barns of the northern portions of the state.

It may be argued that the most significant architectural projects are no longer religious or civic, or even commercial, but are intended to supply entertainment. The money spent on the new football stadium at the Meadowlands might have suggested inclusion in this list merely because its size and cost suggest it must be important. And where is the civic structure erected after 1950 that exudes the brash confidence and optimism in America seen in earlier examples so lovingly restored?

Finally, the impact of commercial architecture upon the landscape after World War II is only suggested. The corporate headquarters became the new American palace. AT&T World Headquarters and the enclave at Giralda Farms in Madison were precursors to the multiplication of the suburban office building throughout the state and justified their existence as isolated structures. The boom in office building lasted until 1987. Sadly, this form of development was corrosive, as it accentuated automobile use, covered pasture and woodland with asphalt, and created temporarily occupied ghettos at the expense of city and town. These structures' horizontal sprawl is in direct contrast to the vertical Goldman Sachs Tower. Though we do not forecast the demise of these office structures, one wonders if their ilk will soon be seen again.

It is likely that more time must pass before we know which of today's trends will, indeed, last. For example, there is no celebratory inclusion of sustainably designed buildings. On the other hand, it is worth noting that every preserved or rehabilitated structure originally built from natural materials extends the life of these aging structures far beyond the life expectancy of most buildings erected in the past fifty years.

Although there are modern buildings included in our list, the absence of the work of many star architects of the late twentieth century is surprising. Projects by Richard Meier and Frank Gehry, both winners of the Pritzker Prize (the Nobel Prize of architecture), are not included, though each has significant built work in New Jersey. Also illuminating is the realization that no new urbanist community is included. This significant planning and development model, now well over thirty years old, seems not to have taken a foothold in New Jersey, in spite of the influence of Radburn and the commuter railroad communities so well executed in the early twentieth century.

In the end, the gauge of architecture is human. The reasons for the selections are idiosyncratic and personal. Though our choices are based on the principles of good design learned throughout a career, there is, without doubt, a sense that the art of the practical is also a standard applied in evaluating buildings and places. It is not easy to have good work realized. No one knows this better than those whose task it is to bring architecture into existence. And so it seems that admiration of good work, as represented here, encompasses recognition of an ability to last, physically and emotionally connected to the community, and an ability to be transformed, through either addition or alternative use.

It is important to reemphasize that even though this book has historical information concerning New Jersey architecture, more is needed. It suggests how fascinating, exciting, expansive, and illuminating such a reference work could be, because New Jersey's architectural heritage is extraordinary.

About the Authors

Philip S. Kennedy-Grant, FAIA, is an architect, artist, and writer. From 1984 to 1993 he was chairman of the editorial board of *Architecture New Jersey* magazine. He has written extensively for *Architecture New Jersey,* as well as for *Architectural Record, Architecture,* and *Texas Architect.* He received a 1989–1990 Fellowship for his writing and editing, and a 1992 Artist in Education grant, both from the New Jersey State Council on the Arts. He has taught architecture at the New Jersey Institute of Technology. His travel sketches have been published nationally and exhibited in Washington, D.C. Since the inception of his architectural practice in 1989, he has been honored frequently by the AIA for the design excellence of his work.

Mark Alan Hewitt, FAIA, is an architect, preservationist, and architectural historian. He has taught architecture at Rice and Columbia Universities, the University of Pennsylvania, and the New Jersey Institute of Technology. Among his publications are *The Architect and the American Country House* and *Gustav Stickley's Craftsman Farms: The Quest for an Arts & Crafts Utopia,* and he coauthored *The Architecture of Carrère & Hastings.* He received Graham Foundation Fellowships in 1985 and 2004, an NEH/ Winterthur senior fellowship in 1996, and a 2008 Arthur Ross Award for his writing on classical architecture. He currently serves on the faculty of the art history department at Rutgers University in New Brunswick, in addition to running his own architectural firm.

Michael J. Mills, FAIA, a principal in Mills + Schnoering Architects, LLC, in Princeton, New Jersey, has devoted more than twenty-five years to the preservation, restoration, and adaptive use of some of the region's most significant historic structures. Mills has served as chair of the advisory group of the AIA Historic Resources Committee and is a past president of Preservation New Jersey, the statewide nonprofit preservation organization.

He has lectured at Princeton University's School of Architecture and Urban Planning, at meetings of the Society for College and University Planning, and at the Association of Preservation Technology's international conference. Publication credits include articles in the *APT Bulletin* and in the journal of the AIA's Academy of Architecture for Justice.

Alexander M. Noble is a professional photographer. He has photographed and written a regular column for *New Jersey Countryside* magazine, had a one-man show of his portraits in 2002, and has won numerous art awards for his photography. He has photographed architecture as both assistant and principal since 2001.

AIA New Jersey Contributors

The responsibility for collating and evaluating nominations for inclusion in this book rested with these members of the AIA New Jersey 150 Committee:

Edward N. Rothe, FAIA, Chairman
Robert F. Barranger, AIA
Kimberly L. Bunn, AIA
Michael Calafati, AIA
Stephen J. Carlidge AIA
Jerome Leslie Eben, AIA
Jerome Morley Larson Sr., AIA

Seth A. Leeb, AIA
Robert Longo, AIA
Yogesh Mistry, AIA
Robin L. Murray, FAIA
Martin G. Santini, FAIA
Bruce D. Turner, AIA

The following AIA New Jersey members made contributions to the 150 project:

Brian W. Ambruster, AIA
John Amelchenko, AIA
Edward A. Arcari, AIA
Architects League of Northern
    New Jersey (Michael Busch Jr.)
Paul Barlo, AIA
Robert F. Barranger, AIA
Ronald P. Bertone, FAIA
Alexander Bol, AIA
Karen M. Bonner, AIA
William M. Brown III, AIA
Ann Butera
Stephen J. Carlidge, AIA
Richard E. Carroll, AIA

AIA Central New Jersey
    (Donna Terzano)
Carmine Cerminara, AIA
Roman N. Chapelsky, AIA
Anthony J. C. Church Sr., AIA
Carol Ciesielski
Skip Cimino
Robert Cozzarelli, AIA
Rafael R. Da Silva, AIA
Joseph B. DeAndrea Jr. AIA
Robert F. DeSantis, AIA
Joseph Diaco, AIA
Suzanne DiGeronimo, FAIA
Judy A. Donnelly, AIA

Peter D. Dorne, AIA
Jerome Leslie Eben, AIA
Robert G. Emert Jr., AIA
Deane Evans, FAIA
Jamil E. Faridy, AIA
Joseph Flock, AIA
Kenneth J. Fox, AIA
Ronald D. Franke, AIA
Verity L. Frizzell, AIA
Tony Gambino
Urs Gauchat, Hon., AIA
Edmund H. Gaunt Jr., AIA
Robert F. Gebhardt, AIA
Richard B. Graham Jr., AIA
Michael Graves, FAIA
Norman Greaves, Assoc. AIA
Emily Hammer
Michael J. Hanrahan, AIA
Robert A. Hazelrigg, AIA
J. Robert Hillier, FAIA
Gerhard Huegel, AIA
Allan W. Kehrt, FAIA
Philip S. Kennedy-Grant, FAIA
Keystone Cement Company
Stacey Ruhle Kliesch, AIA
Ed P. Klimek, AIA
Noboru Kobayashi, AIA
Peter Kozielski, AIA
Thomas F. Lavin, Assoc. AIA
Seth A. Leeb, AIA
Harold Lichtman, AIA
Robert M. Longo, AIA
Leo H. Mahony, AIA
Scott W. McConnell
Thomas D. Meyers, AIA
Justin A. Mihalik, AIA
David Mozes

Robin L. Murray, FAIA
Anthony Naccarato, PE
Raymond Nadaskay, AIA
AIA Newark and Suburban
    Architects
Edward M. O'Brien, AIA
Anthony Pagnotta, AIA
Lawrence Powers, Esq.
Jack A. Purvis, AIA
Frank H. Radey Jr., AIA
James J. Ramentol, AIA
Pamela Lucas Rew, AIA
Peter T. Ricci, AIA
David M. Rosen, AIA
Lloyd A. Rosenberg, AIA
Edward N. Rothe, FAIA
Antonio Scalise
Thomas J. Sharp
Michael Shatken, AIA
George F. Sincox, AIA
Lawrence H. Skott, AIA
Roy Sokoloski, AIA
Scott R. Spiezle, AIA
SWS Architects
Thomas J. Sykes, AIA
Richard P. Tokarski, AIA
Bruce D. Turner, AIA
Barbara E. Vincentsen, AIA
Eric L. Wagner, AIA
Sergie Waisman, AIA
Joseph L. Walker III, Assoc. AIA
AIA West Jersey
Fritz Winterle
Mark E. Yarrington, AIA
David M. Zaiser, AIA
Robert E. Zampolin, AIA

Index

Note: Main entries in **boldface**

Absecon Lighthouse, 130, *133*
Adventure Aquarium (Camden), 136
AIA. *See* American Institute of
  Architects
Alfred M. Heston Collection, 111
Allamuchy State Park, 177
Allen, Augustus, 48
All Faiths Chapel (Manalapan), 84
Allied Chemical and Dye Corporation,
  48
All Saints' Memorial Church
  (Navesink), 77
American classical architecture, 27
American Home Products, 172
American Immigration Museum
  (Ellis Island), 18
American Institute of Architects (AIA),
  1, 4, 77, 83; AIA gold medalist, 34;
  AIA Honor Award, 157–158; AIA New
  Jersey, viii
American Renaissance, 167
American Revolution, vii, 76, 180
Ammann, Othmar H., 11
Antiquities of Athens, The (Stuart and
  Revett), 71
Appalachian: chain, 163; Trail, 178
Arcade (Asbury Park), 86, 87
Arnold Constable department stores,
  44
Art Deco, 22
Art Moderne, 30, 31, 99, 125
Arts and Crafts movement, 176
Asbury Park, *74*, 86–89, 97, 120
**Asbury Park Convention Hall and
  Casino**, 86–87; Casino, *74*
AT&T, 164, 168

AT&T World Headquarters
  (Basking Ridge), *168*, 180
Atlantic City, 50, 95, 97, 108, 110–113,
  115–117, 120, *179*
Atlantic City Race Course
  (Mays Landing), 114
Atlantic County, 3, 116
Atlantic Highlands, 130
Atlantic Ocean, 19, 97, 106
Avalon, 120

Bachman-Wilson House (Millstone),
  166
Bacon, Henry Jr., 64
Bainbridge House (Princeton), 159
Ballinger and Perrot, 138
ballparks, downtown (Trenton,
  Newark, Camden), 161, 162
Baltusrol golf course, 109
Bamberger family, 33
Barnegat, 130
Barnegat Bay Decoy and Baymen's
  Museum, 105
Barnegat Inlet, 106
Barnegat Lighthouse, 130, *132*
Baroque style, 129
Barrett and Bogart, 33
barrier islands, *106*, 120
Bartholdi, Frédéric Auguste, 19
BASCO store, 140
Basie, William "Count," 81
Basking Ridge, 168
Battery Potter (Sandy Hook), 76
Battle of Long Island (Battle of
  Brooklyn), 56
Bayonne, 26

Bayonne Public Library, 26
Beach Haven, 75
Bear Mountain Bridge, 141
Beaux Arts style, 17, 24, 26, 27, 64, 116, 118, 167, 169
Bell Labs (Holmdel), 82
Belleville, 40
Beneficial Corporation, 170
Benjamin, Asher, 165
Benjamin Franklin Bridge, 136
Bergen County, 3, 57, 61
Bergen County Historical Society, 56
Bergen County Militia, 68
Bergenfield, 12
Bernardsville, 171
Betelle, James O., 127
Beyer Blinder Belle, 50
"Black Maria" (Edison National Historic Site), 43
Blair, C. Ledyard, 169
Blair, John Insley, 149
Blair and Company Building, 169
Blairsden (Peapack), 169
Blashfield, Edwin, 24, 27
Bloomfield Hills, Mich., 158
Bluffs, The (Red Bank), 80
B'nai Jeshurun Synagogue (Short Hills), 53
boardwalk, 86, 88, *96*, 97, 108, 110, 115, 119. *See also specific sites*
Boardwalk Hall (Atlantic City), *110*, *179*
Bogota, 12
Bon Jovi, Jon, 89
Borglum, Gutzon, 27, 28
Boring and Tilton, 18, 26
Branch Brook Park (Newark), *33*, 37
Bridgeton, 108, 128–129
Bridgewater, 170
Brite and Bacon, 64
Broad Street (Red Bank), 81
Broad Street Presbyterian Church (Bridgeton), 128
Bronx-Whitestone Bridge, 11
Brooklyn Bridge, 141
Broom, Lewis, 143
Brown, A. Page, 148
Brown, Benjamin, 85
Bulfinch, Charles, 124
Burlington, 77

Burlington County, 3
Burnham, Wilbur Herbert, 151
Burr, Aaron, 16
Button, Stephen Decatur, 123
Byram Township, 177
Byrne, Gov. Brendan, 21

Cady, Josiah William, 174
Cahill, Gov. William, 13
Camden, 134–138, 161
Camden County, 3
Camden Riversharks, 136
Camden Waterfront, 136
Campbell's Field (Camden), 136
Campbell Soup Company, 136
Canoe Brook, 109
Cape May, 107, 108, 121–123, 130
Cape May County, 3
Cape May inns, 122
Cape May Lighthouse, 130, *131*
Cape May National Wildlife Refuge, 108
Capitol Complex. *See* State of New Jersey Capitol Complex
Caribbean Motel (Wildwood), 120
Carlton Theater. *See* Count Basie Theatre
Carmel Retreat Center (Mahwah), 59
Carnegie, Andrew, 40–41, 126
Carnegie libraries: Atlantic City **(Carnegie Library Center of Richard Stockton College of New Jersey)**, 50, *111*; **Bayonne**, 26; **Belleville**, 40; **Camden**, 137; **Kearny**, 41; **Vineland**, 126
Carousel House (Asbury Park), 88
Carrara glass, 125
Carrère, John (Merven), 76, 79, 169
Carrère and Hastings, 5, 33, 64, 79, 83, 178
Carteret, Philip, 28
Casino Building (Asbury Park), *74*, 86–88
Cathedral Basilica of the Sacred Heart (Newark), 32
Cathedral Church of Saint John the Divine (NYC), 32
Central New Jersey Railroad, 69
Central Railroad of New Jersey (CRRNJ), 21
Chambersburg (Trenton), 141

Chapman, Clarence, 59
Chautauqua movement, 44
Chicago, 37
Christie House. *See* James B. Christie
    House
City Beautiful movement, 27, 118
Clairidge Cinema (Montclair), 49
Clam Creek, 113
Clarkson, Dr. William, 128
classical style, 24, 26–27, 31, 40, 43,
    50, 64, 95, 138, 148
Classical Revival, 111, 129
Cliosophical Society, 148
Collegiate Gothic style, 127, 149–150,
    153, 156
Collingswood, 139
Colonial style, 170
Colonial Revival, 73, 76, 170
Colonnade Apartments (Newark), 37
Colt, John and Samuel, 65
Colt Gun Mill (Paterson), 65
Congress for New Urbanism, 61
Congress Hall (Cape May), 122, *123*
Connick, Charles, 151, 153
Constitutional Convention, 54
Continental Congress, 54, 147
Convention Hall and Casino
    (Asbury Park), 86, 87
Cooper's Ferry Development
    Association, 136
Coote, Richard, 15
Cope, Walter, 127, 149–150
Corinthian order, 167
Corner, James, 67
Costello, Elvis, 89
Count Basie Theatre (Red Bank), 81
Cox, Kenyon, 24, 27
Craftsman Farms (Parsippany), 176
Cram, Ralph Adams, 5, 127, 151, 153
Cranbrook Academy Natatorium, 158
CUH2A, 39
Cumberland County, 3, 129
Cumberland County Courthouse
    (Bridgeton), 129
Cummings, Charles, 35

Dana, John Cotton, 34
Danforth, Charles, 64
Danforth Memorial Library. *See*
    Paterson Library

Davis, Alexander Jackson, 45
Davis, McGrath and Kiessling, 41
Deal, 95
de Blois, Natalie, 9
Delaware and Raritan Canal, 141
Delaware Bay, 78, 108, 121, 128, 130
Delaware River, 122, 134, 136, 163;
    Delaware River Port Authority, 136;
    Delaware River Region, 3, 134
Delaware Valley, 125
Delaware Water Gap, 163
Democratic Party convention, 1964,
    110
Devine Park (Spring Lake), 92
Dexter, Lambert and Company, 62
Dey, Dirck, 68
Dey, Theunis, 68
Dey Mansion (Wayne), 68
Dillon's Creek Marina (Island
    Heights), 104
diner. *See* White Manna Diner
Doane, Jonathan, 143
Dobbins, Richard J., 123
Dock's Oyster House (Atlantic City),
    112
Dodge, Geraldine R., 172
Dodge Poetry Festival, 177
Doo Wop, 5, 108; Preservation League,
    120
**Doo Wop Preservation: Caribbean
    Motel** (Wildwood), 120
Doric order, 56, 148, 165
Dougherty, Frank, 112
Dover, 77
Drew University (Madison), 172
Duany, Andrés, 61
Dutch barns, 180
Dutch colonial style, 56

Earhart, Amelia, 30
East Point Lighthouse (Maurice River
    Township), 124
East Rutherford, 13
East Windsor, 145
Eberhardt Hall (NJIT, Newark), 38
Eckert, Cody, 38
École des Beaux Arts, 1, 178
Edison, Thomas Alva, 43–45
Edison Factory and Museum
    (West Orange), 43

Edison National Historic Site, 44
Edwards, Edward I., 24
Edwards, William D., 24
Egyptian ornament, 36
Eiffel, Gustav, 19
Eisenman, Peter, 148
Elberon, 79, 97
Elizabethtown, 28
Ellis Island (Jersey City), *6, 7, 18,* 20, 26
Elmer, Sen. Jonathan, 128
Emlen Physick House (Cape May), 121
English: Gothic Revival, 127; -style, 175
Englishtown, 75
Erie-Lackawanna Railroad, 169
Essex and Sussex Hotel (Spring Lake), 93
Essex County, 3, 33, 51–52
Essex County Courthouse (Newark), 24, *27,* 167
Essex County Parks, 52
EwingCole, 20
Ewing Township, 100, 146

Fair Lawn, 61
Fairleigh Dickinson University (Madison), 172
Fanwood, 69
Fanwood Railroad Station, 69
Far Hills, 164
Farewell Mills Gatsch Architects, 79, 81, 148
Farley, Sen. Frank S., State Marina, 113
Federal style, 70
Finn's Point Range, 130
fire museum. *See* Trenton Fire Headquarters
"Firenze" (house), 79
First Presbyterian Church (Morristown), 174
First Presbyterian Church (Rumson), 79
Flemington, 164–165
Florham on the Fairways (Florham Park), 175
Florham Park, 48, 175
Ford, Col. Jacob, 173
Ford, President Gerald R., 67

Ford Farewell Mills and Gatsch Architects, 27
Ford Mansion, Washington's Headquarters (Morristown), 164, *173*
Fort Hancock (Sandy Hook), 76
Fort Lee, 9, 11
Fort Nonsense (Morristown), 164
Fort Wood. *See* Statue of Liberty
France, 19, 26
Freemasons, 139
French: Gothic, 32; provincial, 48
Furness, Frank, 121

Galloway Township, 109
Garden State Parkway, 75
Garfield, President James, 97
Garret Mountain, 62
Gateway: National Recreation Area, 76; Region, 3, 4, 7
Gehry, Frank, 181
General Chemical Corporation, 48
George Washington Bridge, 8, *10,* 11
Georgian Court University (Lakewood), 98
Georgian style, 54, 68, 98, 128, 147, 173
German barns, 180
Gershwin, George, 36
Giants Stadium, 13
Gilbert, Cass, 11, 27
Giles, Gen. James, 128
Giralda Farms (Madison), 172, 180
Gladstone, 164
Glazier, S. W., 79
Glenmont (West Orange), 44–45
Glen Ridge, 46–47
Gloucester County, 3
Goldman, Lawrence, 29
Goldman Sachs Tower (Jersey City), 23, 180
Goodheart, Allan, 144
Goodhue, Bertram, 127
Goodhue, H. W., 151
Gordon, James Reily, 167
Gothic Revival, 38, 69, 72, 77
Gothic style, 14, 69, 150–151, 153–154, 158
Gould, George Jay, 98
Gould, Jay, 98

Gould Mansion (Georgian Court
   University, Lakewood), 98
Grad Partnership, 143
Graham, Bruce, 9
Grand Central Station (NYC), 86
Graves, Michael, viii, 5, 21, 34, 136, 148
Great Auditorium and Tents (Ocean
   Grove), 90
Great Depression, 59, 85–86
Greater Atlantic City Region and
   Southern Shore Region, 3, 107
Great Falls, 7, 67
Great Falls State Park (Paterson), *66*,
   67
Great Falls/S.U.M. National Historic
   Landmark District, 63
Great Swamp, 168
Greek: (cross plan; temples), 146; Doric,
   41; ornament, 36; Revival, 71, 148
Greystone (Morris Plains), 38
Griffith Music Foundation, 36
Grounds for Sculpture (Hamilton),
   144
Gruzen and Partners, 53
Gruzen Samton, 15
Gualandi, Lou, 177
Guggenheim, Daniel, 79
Guggenheim, Murry, 79, 83
Guilbert, Ernest F., 127
Guilbert and Betelle, 5
Gwathmey, Charles, 148

Hackensack, 14
Hackensack River, 7, 56
Hackensack Water Works (Oradell),
   57
Haddonfield, 135
Hague, Mayor Frank, 22
Hale and Morse, 137
Hamilton, 144
Hamilton, Alexander, 16, 67
Hamilton Farm (Gladstone), 164
Hamilton Park (Weehawken), 16
Hanna/Olin, 73
Harbeson, John, 64
Haskell, Llewellyn, 45
Hastings, Thomas, 76, 79, 169
Hauptmann, Bruno, 165
Hejduk, John, 148
Hell Gate arch bridge, 11

Hertersville Refuge, 124
Highlands, 78, 163
High Point State Park (Sussex), *163*,
   178; Monument, 163, 178
Hill, Frank, 35
Hillier, Robert, 160
Hillier: Architecture, 20, 42, 136,
   159–160; Group, 170, 172
Hindenburg (airship), 103
Historic American Buildings Survey, 128
Historic American Engineering Record,
   63
historic district, 108, 135, 166
historic preservation, 18, 123–124,
   137, 139. 176
Historical Society of Princeton, 159
Hoboken, 15, 17–18, 72
Hoboken Terminal, 17
Hoffmann-La Roche Building One
   (Nutley), 42
Holly, Henry Hudson, 44
Holmdel, 82
Honeywell, 48
Hopewell, 69
Horizon House (Fort Lee), 9
Housing and Mortgage Finance Agency,
   141
Hubbard House (Red Bank), 80
Hubert Parson house (Monmouth
   University, West Long Branch), 83
Hudson, Henry, 106
Hudson County, 3, 22
Hudson County Courthouse
   (Jersey City), 24
Hudson Highlands, 8
Hudson River, 7–9, 11, 15–16, 23
Hudson River School, 7
Hudson Valley, 59–60
Humphrey, Hubert, 110
Hunt, Jarvis, 34
Hunt, Richard Morris, 1, 19
Hunt and Kelly, 140, 143
Hunterdon County, 3, 165
Hunterdon County Courthouse
   (Flemington), 165

immigrants, 18–19, 32, 102
Indiana limestone, 151, 153
industrial revolution, 7
Inner and Outer Coastal Plains, 135

Inness, George, 50
International Center for Public Health (Newark), 39
International: -style, 73; Style, 85
"Invention Factory." *See* Edison Factory and Museum
Ionic order, 50, 98, 126, 129, 167
Ironbound (Newark), 7, 31
Island Beach State Park, 75, 106
Island Heights, 104
Italian: garden, 98; Renaissance palazzo, 35
Italianate, 147
Izenour, Steven, 120

Jackson, 101–102
Jacques Cousteau National Estuarine Research Reserve (Tuckerton), 105
James B. Christie House (Bernardsville), 171
James Rose Center (Ridgewood), 58
Jersey City, 18–24, 72, 143
Jersey City Medical Center, 22
Jersey Devil, 97
Jersey Shore, vii, 76, 79, 89, 97–98, 105, 120, 124
Jersey Shore Folklife Center (Tuckerton), 105
Jett, Joan, 89
Jockey Hollow (Morristown), 164, 171
Johnson, J. Seward, 144
Johnson, Lyndon, 110
Johnson & Johnson, 164
Johnson & Johnson World Headquarters (New Brunswick), 73
Jones, Charles Granville, 40
Jones, Robert Trent, 109

Kahn, Louis I., 5, 85, 146
Kastner, Alfred, 85
Kean, Col. John, 54
Kean University (Union), 54
Kearny, 40
Keely, Patrick C., 72
Kelbaugh, Douglas, 101
Kelly and Gruzen, 9
King, Dr. Martin Luther Jr., 29
King's College Chapel (Cambridge), 151
Kip, Charlotte, 51
Kip, Frederick Ellsworth, 51

Kip's Castle (Montclair/Verona), 51
Kling, Vincent, 168
Knife and Fork Inn (Atlantic City), 112
Kobayashi, Noboru, 99–100
Koetter-Kim Associates, 155
Kuser, Col. Anthony, and Susie Dryden, 178
"Kypsburg." *See* Kip's Castle

Ladder Company 10. *See* Trenton Fire Headquarters
Lafferty, James V., 117
Lakehurst, 103
Lake Marcia, 178
Lake Michigan, 37
Lake Shore Drive apartments (Chicago), 37
Lakewood, 98–99
Lambert, Catholina, 62
Lambert Castle (Paterson), 62
Lambertville, 163
Landis School (Vineland), 127
Landis Theatre (Vineland), 125
Lansdowne Theatre (near Philadelphia), 125
Larson, Jerome Morley Sr., 80, 84, 175
Latrobe, Benjamin, 147
Latz, Mack, Milton, and Evelyn, 112
Leach, Percival, 177
Learning from Las Vegas (Izenour), 120
Le Corbusier, 9, 11
Lederle, Joseph, 78
Lee, Robert, 101
Lee, William, 125
Lehman, William E., 49, 81
Lewis, Clarence McKenzie, 60
Liberty Hall (Union), 54
Liberty Science Center (Jersey City), 20
Liberty State Park (Jersey City), 7, 19–21
lighthouses: **Absecon,** 130, *133*; **Barnegat,** 130, *132*; **Cape May,** 130, *131*; **East Point,** 124; **Sandy Hook**, 130; Sea Girt, 92; **Twin Lights**, *78*, 130
Lincoln, Abraham, seated statue (Newark), 27
Lincoln Memorial, 64
Lincoln Tunnel, 16
Lindbergh kidnapping trial, 165

Lindenthal, Gustav, 11
Livingston, Gov. William, 54
Livingston-Kean family, 54
Llewellyn Park (West Orange), 44, 45
Lockatong argillite, 153
Lockwood, Greene and Company, 110
Long Beach Island, 75, 106
Long Branch, 79
Lord Construction Company, 103
Lord Memorial Fountain (Somerville), 167
Los Angeles, 29
Louis Kahn Bath House. *See* Trenton Bath House and Day Camp Pavilions
Lucy the Margate Elephant, 117

Madison, 170, 172, 180
Magonigle, H. Van Buren, 33
Mahwah, 59
Maloney, Catharine, 95
Maloney, Martin, 95
Manalapan, 84
Manhattan (island), 11, 15–16, 21, 23, 70, 79. *See also* New York City
Mansion House (Cape May), 122
Marconi's wireless telegraph, 78
Margaret Hague Maternity Hospital (Jersey City), 22
Margate, 117
Marquis de Lafayette Hotel (Cape May), 123
Martin, Richard E., 104
Masonic order, Masons, 36
Matawan, 69
Maurice River: Historical Society, 124; Township, 124
Mays Landing, 114
McComb, John Jr., 70
McGreevey, Gov. James, 67
McHarg, Ian, 106
McKim, Charles F., 64, 174
McKim, Mead and White, 5, 31, 50, 79, 167
Meadowlands, vii, 180
Meadowlands Sports Complex (East Rutherford), 13
medieval-revival style, 51
meetinghouses, Quaker, 128, 135
megalopolis, 7, 13
Meier, Richard, 148, 181

Menlo Park, 43
Mercer County, 3
Merck, 164
Meyer, E. F., 123
Mid-Atlantic Center for the Arts and Humanities, 121
Middlesex County, 3
Middletown, 79
Mies van der Rohe, Ludwig, 37
Military Park (Newark), 28
Miller, Lewis, 44
Miller, Mark, 128
Miller, Mina, 44
Millet, Francis, 24
Millstone, 166
Miss America Pageant, 97, 110
Mitten Memorial Hall (Temple University), 125
modern: American architecture, 146; Gothic, 153
modernism, Modernism, 37, 156
modernist style, 42, 73, 82, 148, 154
Monmouth County, 3, 85
Monmouth University Library (West Long Branch), 83
Monopoly, 108, 115
Montclair, 49–51
Montclair Art Museum, 7, 49, *50*
Mori, Eugene, 125
Mori Building (Vineland), 125
Morris Canal, 177
Morris County, 3, 176
Morris Plains, 38
Morristown, 164, 168, 173–174
Morristown Green, 174
Morristown National Historical Park, 164
Moses, Arnold, 143
motels. *See* Doo Wop Preservation: Caribbean Motel
Mount Rushmore, 27
Mount Vernon Hotel (Cape May), 122
Moylan, James, 143
Murchison, Kenneth M., 17
Murray, Capt. Arthur, 76
Museum of Modern Art (NYC), 148
Myers, Barton, 29

National Historic District, 91
National Historic Landmark, 43, 67, 70–71, 176

National Park Service, 43–44, 67, 76, 173
National Register of Historic Places, 77, 85, 117–118, 160, 166
Navesink, 77
Navesink River, 78
Neoclassical style, 41, 53, 143
Newark, 7, 24, 27–39, 127, 135, 161, 167, 177
Newark Airport Administration Building, 30
Newark Bay, 28
Newark Evening Post, 30
Newark Museum, 7, 34
Newark Orphans Asylum, 38
Newark Penn Station, 31
Newark Public Library, 35
Newark Symphony Hall, 36
New Bridge Landing, 56
New Brunswick, 70–73
New England, 174; fishing village, 104
New Haven (Conn.), 28
New Jersey "Dutch," 56
New Jersey Department of Tourism, 2
New Jersey Division of Parks and Forestry, 113
New Jersey History Collection, Newark Public Library, 35
New Jersey Institute of Technology (Newark), 38
New Jersey Performing Arts Center (NJPAC) (Newark), *1*, 7, *29*, 36
New Jersey Regions map, *3*
New Jersey Sports and Exposition Authority, 13
New Jersey State Aquarium. *See* Adventure Aquarium
New Jersey State Botanical Garden (Ringwood), 60
New Jersey State Fairgrounds. *See* Grounds for Sculpture
New Jersey Symphony Orchestra, 36
New Netherland, 28
new urbanist community, 181
New York City, 7, 18, 32, 56. *See also* Manhattan (island)
"New York Five," 148
New York Harbor, 7, 19–20, 76, 78
New York Public Library, 35, 79, 169
New York State, 19

Nichols, Charles, 48
Nichols, Karen, viii
Nichols, William Henry, 48
"Nipper Building." *See* RCA Victor Building
Norman A. Bleshman Regional Day School (Paramus), 55
North Ward (Newark), 33
"Norwood Park" (Rumson), 79
Notman, John, 143, 147
Novartis, 164
Nutley, 42

Ocean City, 116
Ocean City Boardwalk, 119
Ocean City City Hall, 118
Ocean County, 3, 116
Ocean Grove, 90, *91*, 119; Camp Meeting Association, 91
O'Conner, Francis, 27
Olmsted, Frederick Law, 33, 52
Olmsted Brothers, 33, 52, 178
Olmstedian style, 33
One Airport Road (Lakewood), 100
One Port Center (Camden), 136
Oradell, 57
O'Rourke, Jeremiah, 32

PA Technology Center (East Windsor), 145
Palisades, vii, 8, 11, 16, 22
Palisades Interstate Park, 8
Palladian style, 173
Paramount Theatre (Asbury Park), 86–87
Paramus, 55
Park Theater building (Newark), 35
Parris, Alexander, 124
Parsippany–Troy Hills, 176
Passaic County, 3
Passaic County Courthouse, 64
Passaic County Historical Society, 62
Passaic River, 7, 28, 29, 31, 67, 171
Passaic watershed, 60
Patent Arms Manufacturing Company, 65
Paterson, 7, 16, 62–67, 72, 135
Paterson Library, 64
Paterson Museum, 63
Pavilion apartment tower (Newark), 37

Payette Associates, 157
Peabody and Stearns, 21
Peapack, 169–170
Pedder, Henry C., 44
Pei, I. M., 73
Pelli, Cesar, 23
Pennington, 69
Pennsylvania Railroad, 11, 31
Pennsylvania stone, 151
Pfizer, 164, 170
Pfizer Headquarters (Peapack), 170
Philadelphia, 120, 122, 136–137
Phillipsburg, 21, 177
Physick, Dr. Emlen, 121
Physick House. *See* Emlen Physick
   House
physiographic regions: Ridge, Valley,
   Highlands, Piedmont, 163
Piano, Renzo, 145
Pine Barrens, 135
Pinelands, 105, 134
Pine Valley, 109
planned (residential) community, town,
   44–45, 61, 85, 91
Plater-Zyberk, Elizabeth, 61
Pleasantdale Chateau (West Orange),
   48
Point Pleasant Boardwalk, 96
Pope, John Russell, 60, 164, 167
Port Authority of New York and New
   Jersey, 11, 30
Port Imperial Ferry Terminal
   (Weehawken), 15
Port of New York Authority, 11
Post Office (Lakewood), 99
Potter, Col. David, 128
preservation, 18, 123–124, 137, 139, 176
Price, Bruce, 98
Princeton, vii, 134, 147–160
Princeton Public Library, 159
Princeton University, vii, 147–157, 178;
   Blair Hall, *149*, 150; Butler College,
   156; Cleveland Memorial Tower, 153;
   College of New Jersey, 147; Dillon
   Gymnasium, 150; **Feinberg Hall**,
   158; **Firestone Library Addition**,
   155; **Graduate College**, *152*, 153;
   Lewis Thomas Laboratory, 157;
   Little Hall, 150; **Nassau Hall**, *147*,
   148; North Court, 153; Procter Hall,
   153; **Robertson Hall**, 154; School of
   Public and International Affairs, 154;
   University Chapel, 151; Van Dyke
   Library, 153; **Whig Hall**, *134*, *148*;
   Woodrow Wilson School, 154;
   Wu Hall, 156
Pritzker Prize (Nobel Prize of
   architecture), 181
Prudential Hall. *See* New Jersey
   Performing Arts Center
Public Health Research Institute
   (Newark), 39
Puritans, 28
Pyle, Howard, 24

Quail Hill Boy Scout Camp
   (Manalapan), 84
Quakers, 135
Queen Anne style, 44, 80

Radburn (Fair Lawn), *61*, 181
Rahway River, 8
Ramapo Mountains, 60
Ramapo River Valley, 59
Rankin and Kellogg, 35
Raritan River, 169
RCA Victor, 136
RCA Victor Building (Camden), 138
Red Bank, 80–81
Reservoir Park. *See* Branch Brook Park
Revett, Nicholas, 71
Revolutionary War, 54, 56, 68, 70, 128,
   135, 147, 164
Richard Stockton College of New
   Jersey, 111
Ridgefield Park Station, 12
Ridgewood, 58
Ringwood, 60
River Edge, 56
roadside architecture, 108
Roaring Run sandstone, 151
Roberts, Hugh, 24
Robeson, Paul, 160
Roche-Dinkeloo, 82
Roebling, John, 141
Roebling, Washington, Ferdinand, and
   Charles, 141
Roebling cable, 141
Roebling Complex (Trenton), 141
Rogers, Richard, 5, 145

Rogers Locomotive Works
(Paterson), 63
Roman: arches, 12; brick, 137
Romanesque style, 43
Roosevelt, Franklin D., 85
Roosevelt Planned Community, 85
Rose, James, 58
Ross, Albert R., 50, 111
Rothe, Edward N., ix
Rothe Johnson, 55
Rowland, John T., 22
Rumson, 79, 95
Rutgers, Col. Henry, 70
Rutgers University, 70–71, 73, 105;
    Old Observatory, 71; **Old Queens**,
    70, 71; Queens College, 70; Rutgers
    Scientific School, 71
Ryle, Mary Danforth, 64
Ryle, William, 64

Saarinen, Eero, 5, 82
Saint Catharine Church (Spring
    Lake), *94*, 95
Saint John's Church (Dover), 77
Saint Mary's Episcopal Church
    (Burlington), 77
**Saint Mary's Russian Orthodox
    Church** (Jackson), 102
Saint Peter's Church (Morristown), 174
**Saint Peter's Roman Catholic
    Church** (New Brunswick), 72
Saint Vladimir's Orthodox cemetery
    (Jackson), 102
Saints Peter and Paul Church
    (Williamsburg), 72
Salaam Temple. *See* Newark Symphony
    Hall
Salem County, 3
Sandy Hook, 75–76, 78, 130
Sandy Hook Lighthouse, 130
Sanofi-Aventis, 164
Santini, Martin, ix
Sasaki, Walker and Associates, 82
Scamozzi capitals, 137
Scottish Rite Auditorium
    (Collingswood), 139
Sea Girt, 92
Sea Girt lighthouse, 92
Seaview Marriott (Galloway
    Township), 109

Second Empire style, 80
Sedgewick Theatre (near Philadelphia),
    125
Segal, George, 144
Shadow Lawn (Monmouth University,
    West Long Branch), 83
Shahn, Ben, 85
Shaw, Charles, 121
Shenandoah (navy airship), 103
Shilowitz, Charles, 26
Shingle Style, 79
Shore Region, 3, 75
"Shore, The," 106
Short & Ford & Partners, Architects, 167
Short & Ford/Johnson Jones, 143
Short Hills, 53
Shrewsbury, 92
Shriners, 36
Sieber, Arthur E., 14
Sisters of Mercy, 98
Skidmore, Owings and Merrill, 9
Skylands Manor (Ringwood), 60
Skylands Region, 3, 163–164
Sloan, Samuel, 143
Smith, Robert, 147
Smith, Vivian, 116, 118
Smith, Willard, 71
Society for Establishing Useful
    Manufactures (S.U.M.), 63, 65, 67
Solar Village (Jackson), 101
Somerset County, 3, 167
Somerset County Courthouse
    (Somerville), 167
Somerset Hills, 169
Somerville, 164, 167
Sourland Mountains, vii
South Orange, 53
Southside Johnny and the Asbury
    Jukes, 89
Spalding, George, 57
Spring Lake, 75, *92*, 93–95, 120
Springsteen, Bruce, 89
Starlux motel (Wildwood), *107*
State and National Registers of Historic
    Places, 17, 21, 24, 128
state historic site, 78
State Marina (Atlantic City), 113
**State of New Jersey Capitol
    Complex** (Trenton), *142*, 143;
    Assembly Chamber, 143; Senate

Chamber, 143; State House, 143; State House Annex, 143; State Library, 143; State Museum, 143; State Theatre, 81
Statue of Liberty (Jersey City), 19
Steele's Fudge Shop (Atlantic City), 112
Steel Pier (Atlantic City), 112, 115
Stein, Clarence, 61
Steuben, Baron von, 56
Steuben House (River Edge), 56
Stewardson, John, 127, 149, 150
Stickley, Gustav, 176
Stone Harbor, 120
Stone Pony, The (Asbury Park), 89
Streamlined Moderne, 31
Stuart, James "Athenian," 71
Stuart Richardson House (Glen Ridge), *46*, 47
Substance of Gothic, The (Cram), 153
S.U.M (Society for Establishing Useful Manufactures), 63, 65, 67
Susquehanna Bank Center (Camden), 136
Sussex, 178
Sussex County, 3, 178
Swartout, Edgarton, 167

Teaneck, 12
Temple of the Scottish Rite. *See* Scottish Rite Auditorium
Temple of the Winds (Athens), 71
Temple University, 125
Tiffany: glass, 17; studios, 27
Tilton, Edward L., 26
Tinnicum Island Rear Range, 130
Tracy, Everts, 167
Treat, Robert, 28
Trenton, 134–135, 140–143, 161
Trenton Bath House and Day Camp Pavilions (Ewing Township), 146
Trenton Fire Headquarters, 140
Trenton Jewish Community Center, 146
Trumbauer, Horace, 83, 95
Tsien, Billie, 158
Tucker's Island Lighthouse, 105
Tuckerton Seaport, 105
Tudor style, 60, 116, 150
Turkevitch, Metropolitan Leonty, 102
Turner, Charles Yardley (also C. Y.), 24, 27

Turner, Harold, 171
Tweeter Center (Camden), 136
Twin Lights Lighthouse (Highlands), 78, 130

U.S. Bicentennial, 21
U.S. Centennial, 19
U.S. Declaration of Independence, 19
U.S. Equestrian Team Foundation, 164
U.S. Professional Golf Association, 164
UMDNJ Medical School, 39
Union, 54
Union County, 3
University Heights (Newark), 37; Science Park, 39
Upjohn, Richard, 77; *Upjohn's Rural Architecture*, 77
Upjohn, Richard Mitchell, 1, 77
Usonian style, 47, 166, 171

Valley Forge, Pa., 173
Van Rensselaer, Stephen, 70
Ventnor, 116
Ventnor City Hall, 116
Venturi, Robert, 5, 140, 156–157
Venturi, Scott Brown and Associates, 140
Verizon, 164
Vermont marble, 148
Verona, 51
Verona Park, 52
Verrazano-Narrows Bridge, 11
Victorian style, 80, 91–92, 107, 121–123, 165
Ville Radieuse, 9
Vineland, 125–127
Vineland High School, 127
Vitale and Geiffert, 60

Wallkill Valley, 178
Warren and Wetmore, 86
Warren County, 3
Washington, D.C., 64
Washington, George, 56, 68, 135, 164, 171
Washington Park (Newark), 35
Washington's Headquarters, Ford Mansion (Morristown), 164, *173*, 176
Watchung Mountains, 28

Waterloo Village (Byram Township), 177

Watson and Huckel, 129

Waxwood, Howard B. Jr., 160

Waxwood, The (Princeton), 160

Wayne, 68

Weehawken, 15–16

Welch, John, 38

West, Andrew Fleming, 153

West Long Branch, 83

West Orange, 43–45, 48

Whig Society, 148

White, Lawrence Grant, 31

White, Stanford, 31, 79

White Manna Diner (Hackensack), 14

Whitman, Walt, 136

Wildwood, 5, 97, 107, 108, 120

Wilkes, Kevin, 144

Willet, Henry, 151

Willet Studio, 153

William J. Brennan Courthouse (Jersey City), 24, *25*

Williams, Tod, 158

Wilson, Woodrow, 153

Wire Mill #4. *See* Roebling Complex

Wissahickon schist, 153

Witherspoon, John, 160

Witherspoon, John, neighborhood (Princeton), 160

Witherspoon School for Colored Children. *See* Waxwood, The

Woodbury, 135

Woolworth Building (NYC), 103

Works Progress Administration, 99

World Trade Center (NYC), 154

World War I, 34, 141

World War II, 86, 102, 110, 114, 135, 180

Wright, Frank Lloyd, 5, 47, 166, 171

Wright, Henry, 61

Wyeth, Marion Sims, 5, 178

Wyeth (company), 164, 170, 172

Wyeth Headquarters (Madison), 172

Yamasaki, Minoru, 154

Zabriskie, Jan, 56

Zeppelin Hangar Number One (Lakehurst), 103